TENNESSEE BEGINNINGS

TENNESSEE BEGINNINGS

combining

A Short Description of the
Tennessee Government.
[by Daniel Smith]
— 1793 —
The Constitution of the State of Tennessee.
— 1796 —

and

A Catechetical Exposition of the
Constitution of the State of Tennessee.
by Willie Blount
— 1803 —

The Reprint Company, *Publishers*
Spartanburg, S.C.
1974

Reprinted: 1974, 1976
The Reprint Company, Publishers
Spartanburg, South Carolina 29304

ISBN 0-87152-152-0
Library of Congress Catalog Card Number: 74-583
Manufactured in the United States of America on long-life paper.

Library of Congress Cataloging in Publication Data
Main entry under title:

Tennessee beginnings.

The 1st and 2d works are listed in Evans as 26168 and 31278, respectively.

1. Tennessee—Constitutional law. 2. Tennessee—Politics and government—To 1865. I. Smith, Daniel, 1748–1818. A short description of the Tennassee government. 1974. II. Tennessee. Constitution. The constitution of the State of Tennessee. 1974. III. Blount, Willie, 1767–1835. A catechetical exposition of the constitution of the State of Tennessee. 1974.
KFT402.T45   342'.768'029   74-583
ISBN 0-87152-152-0

ACKNOWLEDGEMENTS

For *Tennessee Beginnings*—a combination of Daniel Smith's *A Short Description of the Tennassee Government*; *The Constitution of the State of Tennessee*, 1796; and Willie Blount's *A Catechetical Exposition of the Constitution of the State of Tennessee*—we have elected to set new type for each volume rather than reproduce them in facsimile editions. Therefore, the size and pagination of each volume in this edition will vary from the original since the new type is larger than that in which the books were originally set. The facsimiles of the three title pages which are included are not necessarily actual original size but have been reduced or enlarged for uniformity. We have, however, made no attempt to correct or edit the originals in the hope that this edition will read exactly as the originals read.

We wish to thank Mr. John Dobson, Special Collections Librarian, University of Tennessee Library, Knoxville, who provided photocopies of the *Constitution* and *Catechetical Exposition* from which we set type. Additionally, Mr. Dobson wrote a new introduction for this edition. Mr. Robert M. McBride, Editor, *Tennessee Historical Quarterly*, provided a copy of *A Short Description* from an original edition in the Tennessee State Library and Archives, Nashville.

The facsimiles of the original title pages are from *Some Tennessee Rarities*, compiled by Ronald R. Allen and privately printed in 1973 in Knoxville. The "Map of the Tennassee Government, Formerly Part of North Carolina," is a reprint of a 1938 reproduction of the first map of the present state of Tennessee.

THE REPRINT COMPANY

INTRODUCTION

Publication of this volume brings together three of the rarest and most unobtainable items of Tennesseana. Daniel Smith's *A Short Description of the Tennassee Government*, *The Constitution of the State of Tennessee* (1796), and Willie Blount's *A Catechetical Exposition of the Constitution of the State of Tennessee* have until now been available only to the very few. Less than a dozen copies of the original Daniel Smith work have been located, just two copies of the Knoxville printing of the Constitution are recorded, and only five locations are known for the original Willie Blount title. The initial piece was issued to accompany the first map of Tennessee and as such was the first work on Tennessee; the second was the earliest printing of Tennessee's first Constitution; and the third, the first Tennessee textbook, was designed to clarify points in the state's first constitution. All three works are credited to highly acclaimed men, all were issued from important early presses, and all now are considered exceedingly valuable books.

Daniel Smith (1748-1818), a native of Stafford County, Virginia, was educated at William and

Mary College and, like many distinguished men of his time, became a surveyor. In the work of this profession he was so accurate that it is said his surveys never needed correction. In 1774 he prepared a map of the headwaters of the tributaries of the Tennessee River, or, as it was then called, the Holston, which is of great service in locating the creeks and rivers of the borderland between southwest Virginia and northeast Tennessee. It was probably because of his proficiency in this that he was selected as a Commissioner of Virginia to extend the line between that state and North Carolina, which had been previously run by Jefferson and others. Within a few years Daniel Smith removed to the Cumberland region, with which he was afterwards definitely associated. In the new country he made the chief surveys for "Map of the Tennassee Government, Formerly Part of North Carolina," published by Matthew Carey, Philadelphia, 1793, the first map of the present state of Tennessee.

Smith at once became a man of prominence in his adopted home. In 1785 he was one of the Trustees named in the act incorporating Davidson Academy. In 1787 he was one of the Justices named in the first court organized in Sumner County (when Sumner was subsequently divided, the newly created county was called Smith in his honor), and in 1788 he was appointed Brigadier General of Mero District. In 1790 he was appointed Secretary of the Territory of the United States South of the River Ohio by George Washington, and during his term of office (1790–1796) was frequently Acting Governor. He was also Acting Treasurer of the Territory, 1792–1794. He was one of the delegates from Sumner County to the Convention of 1796 called for the purpose of forming a Constitution or permanent form of government for Tennessee. This Convention sat twenty-seven days and framed a Constitution which remained unaltered until 1834. He was elected by the first Legislature of Tennessee as one of the four presidential electors. In 1798 he was appointed to the United States Senate to fill the vacancy caused by the resignation of Andrew Jackson, and was again Senator from 1805 until his resignation in 1809.

After his retirement from public life, Smith's remaining years were spent in developing the estate in Sumner County he had acquired many years earlier and on which in 1794 he had built Rock Castle, a house constructed of cut stone which is even today a showplace of Middle Tennessee. François André Michaux, a French botanist who passed through Tennessee in 1802, wrote in his *Travels to the Westward of the Allegany Mountains* (London, 1805)

> On the road we stopped with... among others, General Smith, one of the oldest inhabitants of this country, where he has resided sixteen

or seventeen years. America is indebted to him for the best map of this state, which is to be found in the *Geographical Atlas*, published by Matthew Carey, a bookseller at Philadelphia. He acknowledged, however, that this map, which has been some years laid down, is imperfect in many points. The general is possessed of a fine estate, cultivated in maize and cotton: he has also a well-conducted distillery, where he makes peach brandy, which he sells for a piaster per gallon. He employs his leisure in chemistry. I observed that he had English translations of the works of Lavoisier and Foureroy.

Smith was well known for his work as a surveyor and for his early map of Tennessee, but whether he actually wrote *A Short Description of the Tennassee Government. . . To Accompany and Explain a Map of that Country* has been questioned. Although the rare pamphlet has generally been attributed to him, there is no statement of authorship on the piece and no record is to be found showing that the text came from Smith's hand. Most references cautiously place Smith's name as author in brackets, which in itself is an indication of doubt. Regardless of who wrote it, the work was popular, which is testified to by the four editions issued before 1800. Both Sabin's *Dictionary of Books Relating to America* and Evans' *American Bibliography* show the 1793 edition to have been issued without the map. Evans suggests the map referred to was the one engraved for Carey's American edition of Guthrie's *Geography*. He indicates that such copies as have the map obtained it from that source, published a year or more later than the date of the text. Two editions appeared in 1796 with revisions and with slightly altered titles (one boasting the addition of the Tennessee Constitution). An edition essentially like that of 1796 appeared in 1797, as well as a reprint of the same text in Imlay's *A Topographical Description of the Western Territory*. At about the same time there was also a French edition. In 1936 a special photostat limited edition (15 copies) was issued by the Massachusetts Historical Society, using the American Antiquarian Society's copy.

The 1793 edition of Smith's *A Short Description of the Tennassee Government. . .* reprinted here came originally from the press of Matthew Carey, the celebrated late 18th and early 19th century editor, author and publisher of Philadelphia. In the early days of American publishing, most publishers were satisfied to reprint the work of established English authors, but Carey, who was unique in his field, gave encouragement to American writers and offered them through his book-publishing business an outlet for their work. He was a powerful influence in developing a reading class throughout the country. The rare little volume attributed to Smith and made available to the public by Carey has become of prime importance because it was the first printed work relating to the present Tennessee. This importance is reflected by the sales records established for it. In 1938 the New York firm of Edward Eberstadt & Son offered the 1793 edition for $250, in 1953 the same firm offered a copy for $450, and in 1967 Parke-Bernet Galleries sold a copy of the 1796 edition for $1,800.

The *Constitution of the State of Tennessee* was drawn by a convention of men gathered at Knoxville in January and February of 1796. The group included five delegates from each of the eleven counties of which Tennessee was then composed. Among them were such notable figures as Andrew Jackson, James Robertson, Joseph McMinn, William Cocke, Archibald Roane, James White, William Blount, Daniel Smith, and Landon Carter. Members of this Constitutional Convention demonstrated their qualifications for framing the instrument of government by going on to hold some of the highest offices in the land. Andrew Jackson became President, Archibald Roane and Joseph McMinn became Governors and William Blount, William Cocke, and Daniel Smith became U.S. Senators.

The Tennessee Constitution is known to have been printed several times in the year it was adopted. A resolution of the Constitutional Convention dated

February 6, 1796, directed the state printer (George Roulstone) to print fifty copies of the Constitution. The *American Imprints Inventory* notes a printing issued without a title-page (perhaps at Knoxville) as well as the Roulstone imprint of 1796. Both the small number of copies issued and the significance of the pioneer printer contribute to the exceedingly high value now placed on the first impressions. Another printing was issued at Philadelphia by Thomas Condie in the same year and it was an added feature of a 1796 edition of Daniel Smith's work. It was again offered by Roulstone at Knoxville in 1799, this time prefixed to the Constitution of the United States.

Although records show copies of the 1796 Roulstone Constitution among the holdings of both the Henry E. Huntington Library and the New York Public Library, only the New York Public Library copy can now be located.

The author of *A Catechetical Exposition*, Willie Blount (pronounced Wiley) was the younger half-brother of William Blount, Governor of the Territory South of the River Ohio. He was born in Bertie County, North Carolina, in 1797 or 1798 and was educated at the institutions that later became Columbia and Princeton Universities. Around the year 1790 he followed his brother to the Tennessee country and served for a time as one of his secretaries. The youthful secretary was immediately thrown into the activities of state-craft, with personal and official contact with the leaders in the new country. He was associated with such notable men as Andrew Jackson, John Sevier, James White, Samuel Carrick, Samuel Doak, and Archibald Roane. He was licensed to practice law in 1794, and before reaching thirty years of age was elected a judge of the Superior Court of Tennessee, but declined the office. About 1802 he settled in Montgomery County and, beginning with the 1807 term, represented that county in the state legislature. He had been a charter trustee of Blount College (forerunner of the University of Tennessee) in 1794 and served as a trustee of Cumberland College, 1809-1815. In 1809 he was elected governor and was reelected in 1811 and in 1813. The gubernatorial service for which he is best remembered was the prompt and valuable assistance extended to General Andrew Jackson in the campaigns against the Creek Indians. Through an appeal to the Tennessee Legislature, he was allowed to call for thirty-five hundred volunteers who were to be supported by an appropriation of $370,000. For his sustaining actions in this conflict, Governor Blount received expressions of gratitude from President James Madison and three Secretaries of War, and a commendatory resolution by the Tennessee Legislature. Again, when war with England occurred in 1812, he immediately made available to President Madison twenty-five hundred volunteers under the command of General Andrew Jackson. He was candidate for Governor against Sam Houston in 1827, but was badly defeated. The year before his death in 1835 he was a delegate from Montgomery County to Tennessee's second Constitutional Convention.

It may be conjectured that Willie Blount's detailed knowledge of the Tennessee Constitution was a result of having worked closely with his brother, William Blount, during the term of the initial Constitutional Convention. William Blount was president of the Convention and Willie Blount, sometimes acting as his brother's secretary, would have been well acquainted with the provisions of the Constitution. The publication of *A Catechetical Exposition*, no doubt, came about because of his special association with the actual development of the Constitution. It is arranged as a series of questions and answers and was designed to explain the many points encompassed by the document. The question and answer format, as well as the title-page phrase "Intended principally for the use of schools," accounts for its being called the first Tennessee textbook.

As previously noted, the first printing of *The Constitution of the State of Tennessee* was done at Knoxville in 1796 by George Roulstone, the first printer in Tennessee. Roulstone also printed Blount's short work on the Constitution, advertised in the *Knoxville Gazette* of January 26, 1803, as "Just Published (price 25 cents) for sale at the printing office. . . ." Roulstone, who established the *Knoxville Gazette* (Tennessee's first newspaper) in 1791, was well known to the younger Blount. While Blount was secretary to the Governor, Roulstone was Clerk of the Territorial Council and Public Printer, and the two served at the same time as trustees of Blount College. If for no other reason, *A Catechetical Exposition* would be a significant piece simply because it is one of the scarcest products to have come from Roulstone's Knoxville press. Any Roulstone imprint is a rare and valuable item, but this most unusual compilation from the hand of Willie Blount is exceptionally esteemed. It is almost never seen and has never been separately reprinted. The copy held by The University of Tennessee is bound with *Laws of the State of Tennessee*, also printed by George Roulstone at Knoxville in 1803. Other known copies were apparently issued separately. In addition to the one at Tennessee, copies have been reported only by the Henry E. Huntington Library, the Library of Congress, the Memphis Public Library, and the University of Texas. Since no sale has been recorded, an established value for this small work cannot be quoted. Even so, its monetary worth is unquestionably substantial and its historical consequence is undoubted.

The combination of Daniel Smith's description

of the Tennessee country and Willie Blount's exploration of its instrument of government, accompanied by that instrument of government, is an appropriate union. One provides the earliest printed look at a newly opened territory, complete with accounts of topographical and navigational features, climatic conditions, natural resources, settlements, population, distances from place to place, agricultural and industrial potential, aboriginal inhabitants, historic events, and form of government. The others, complementing the first, present the emerging state's constitution (a constitution so sound that it stood without change for thirty-eight years) and, in simple form, a complete analysis of it. That these important pieces of Tennesseana, virtually unknown because of rarity, are now readily available is a noteworthy development.

Daniel Smith's *Short Description of the Tennassee Government* is listed in *The Library of Congress Catalog of Printed Cards*, (Ann Arbor, 1945), numbers 2-16019, 6-44004, and A31-1196; Charles Evans' *American Bibliography* (Chicago, 1925), numbers 26168, 31199, and 31200; Joseph Sabin's *Bibliotheca Americana, A Dictionary of Books Relating to America* (New York, 1892-1928) numbers 82420, 82421, and 82422; Edward Eberstadt's *The Annotated Eberstadt Catalogs of Americana* (New York, 1965), numbers 113:398 and 131:644; Wright Howes'

U.S.iana (New York, 1962), number S–587; Parke-Bernet Galleries' *The Celebrated Collection of Americana Formed by the Late Thomas Winthrop Streeter* (New York, 1967), number 1633; and Ronald Allen's *Some Tennessee Rarities* (Knoxville, 1973), number 4. *The Constitution of the State of Tennessee* (Knoxville, 1796) is listed in Charles Evans' *American Bibliography*, number 31278; Joseph Sabin's *Bibliotheca Americana*, number 94729; Douglas McMurtrie's *Early Printing In Tennessee*, number 14; *American Imprints Inventory*, number 32, *A Check List of Tennessee Imprints, 1793–1840* (Chicago, 1942), number 14; and Ronald Allen's *Some Tennessee Rarities*, number 7. Willie Blount's *A Catechetical Exposition of the Constitution of the State of Tennessee: Intended Principally for the Use of Schools* is listed in *The Library of Congress Catalog of Printed Cards*, (Ann Arbor, 1943), number 2–11338; *American Imprints Inventory*, number 32, *A Check List of Tennessee Imprints, 1793–1840*, number 42; Joseph Sabin's *Bibliotheca Americana*, number 6004; Douglas McMurtrie's *Early Printing in Tennessee* (Chicago, 1933), number 37; and Ronald Allen's *Some Tennessee Rarities*, number 12.

December 1973 JOHN DOBSON
Special Collections Librarian
University of Tennessee

A

SHORT DESCRIPTION

OF THE

TENNASSEE GOVERNMENT,

OR THE

TERRITORY

OF THE

UNITED STATES

SOUTH OF THE RIVER OHIO,

TO ACCOMPANY AND EXPLAIN A
MAP OF THAT COUNTRY.

PHILADELPHIA:

PRINTED BY MATHEW CAREY, BOOKSELLER,
No. 118, HIGH-STREET.

—1793.—

A

SHORT DESCRIPTION

OF THE

TENNASSEE GOVERNMENT,

OR THE

TERRITORY

OF THE

UNITED STATES

SOUTH OF THE RIVER OHIO,

TO ACCOMPANY AND EXPLAIN A
MAP OF THAT COUNTRY.

PHILADELPHIA:
Printed by MATHEW CAREY, Bookseller,
No. 118, High-street.

—1793.—

A

SHORT DESCRIPTION, &c.

THE Tennassee government, or the territory of the United States, south of the river Ohio, is that tract of country, which was ceded to the United States by the state of North-Carolina, in the year 1789. It is situated between the parallels of 35 degrees and 36 degrees 30 minutes, extending from the great Iron mountain to the river Mississippi.

WHEN we cast our eyes on the map of any country, especially the map of a new country, in which little else is seen than the situation of mountains, rivers, and plains, we are desirous to know what is the state of its soil and climate; what are the advantages its inhabitants may be expected to enjoy, or the difficulties under which they must labour. A general answer to these questions, as they respect the Tennassee government, is the object of this publication.

We discover, at first sight, that the southern territory is cut into eastern and western divisions, by Cumberland mountain, a ridge near thirty miles broad; and it is probable, that the commercial connexions of people who live in the eastern division, may be different from those of the western inhabitants. The great island on Holston river, is not above 340 miles from Richmond in Virginia, along a good waggon road, whence we may conclude that the settlers on Holston will preserve a considerable intercourse with the Atlantic states; but people who live to the westward of Cumberland mountain, will send their produce to market by means of the Mississippi. This remarkable difference in their situation will probably induce the inhabitants of those districts to employ themselves differently, for the most proper or profitable productions in one settlement, may not be most profitable in the other.

The Holston settlement contains 28,649 inhabitants, though in the year 1775 it hardly contained 2000. The land in this settlement is generally fertile; but the face of the country is much broken. Placed, as it is, between two large mountains, we may readily suppose that the farmer never suffers by the want of rain. The soil produces wheat, barley, Indian corn, hemp, and flax, in great perfection. Physicians have not hitherto found their way to that country, for the people have not been sick. They enjoy a temperate climate, ease, and abundance.

Iron ore abounds in that country. A capital furnace and forge have lately been erected on Holston, near the Virginia line. There is a bloomery below the mouth of Wataga, and another 25 miles above the mouth of French Broad. There are also sundry leadmines in the settlement, one in particular on French Broad river, that produces seventy five per cent in pure lead.

The greatest part of the Tennassee government lies on the west side of Cumberland mountain; and though that country has hardly been settled ten years by civilized men, it naturally claims the greatest share of our attention, because it is extensive, and will probably become the residence of a numerous and powerful colony.

The mean distance between Cumberland mountain and the Mississippi is about 230 miles. This, at 103 miles broad, gives fifteen millions of acres; and it is generally agreed, that eleven or twelve millions of that land may be cultivated to advantage; such is the proportion of arable land. The natives, who formerly inhabited that country, must have been very numerous; we seldom go more than five or six miles along the banks of Cumberland river, without finding a large burying-place, the evident remains of a considerable town. As the Indians had their choice of land, and do not appear to have been equally numerous in other places, we may suppose they found this to be a soil on which they could live with greatest ease.

Of the Rivers.

FROM the face of the map it appears, that this country is well intersected by rivers, and most of those rivers are navigable by large boats; some of them by ships.

TENNASSEE river is navigable by vessels of great burden to the Muscle Shoals; those shoals are only to be passed in small boats or batteaux; from the Muscle Shoals the river is navigable in boats of 40 or 50 tons burden, to the Virginia line.

CUMBERLAND river is navigable in large vessels to Nashville, and thence in boats to the mouth of Obas river.

DUCK river is navigable in boats about 90 miles. The waters of Harpath, Cany-fork, Stones, Roaring and Red river, have uniformly a gentle current towards the mouth, whence they are all navigable in boats for a considerable distance. In a word, no spot can be marked in that country, that is more than 20 miles from a boatable stream, so great are its advantages of water-conveyance.

THERE are five navigable rivers in this territory which discharge themselves immediately into the Mississippi, viz. Wolf, Hatchee, Forked-deer, Obion, and Reelfoot.

WOLF river, seven miles from the mouth, is about 50 yards wide; Hatchee 80 yards; Forked-deer 60 yards; Obion 70 yards; and Reel-foot 30 yards. These rivers in general are deep, and flow with a gentle current, unincumbered with rocks or rapids, until they reach the barren or broken tract in which they rise. Each of those rivers is bordered by a small strip of low ground, 60 or 80 yards wide, and this again is terminated by a gentle slope or secondary bank. In order to understand the use, perhaps the cause of this remarkable circumstance, an inner and an outer bank to each of those rivers, it should be remembered that the river Mississippi, during the month of May, rises perpendicularly near 25 feet, at which season the low ground on both sides of that river is covered with water, to the depth of 12 or 18 inches. This inundation, on the west side of the river extends to a great distance, for the country seems to be lower in that direction, and some of the waters of that river find their way to the ocean by other channels. On the east side of the river, the inundation hardly extends above five miles; at that distance the waters are restrained by a secondary bank, which runs parallel to the general course of the river. This outer bank is properly the beginning of high and dry land. It is obvious, that during those spring floods, the rivers, which run into the Mississippi, most suffer a considerable interruption. Their current is affected 10, 15, or 20 miles from the mouth, and they overflow their banks. On those occasions, the secondary bank of those small rivers becomes necessary, for it prevents the adjacent land from being overflowed, except the narrow border above described. The industry of a small French colony at New Orleans has given a sufficient proof that the inundations of the Mississippi may be restrained by artificial banks, by which means arable land has been and may be secured, that is hardly equalled in value by any known lands, except in Egypt.

Of the Timber, Plants, Animals, &c.

THE land on the waters of Tennassee and Cumberland rivers is generally well timbered. In some places, there are glades of rich land without timber; but these are not frequent nor large. The general growth is poplar, hickory, black-walnut, buck-eye, or the horse-chesnut, sycamore, locust, and the sugar-maple. The under growth, in many places, is cane 15 or 20 feet high, so close together, as to exclude all other plants; where the cane does not abound, we find red-bud, wild-plumb, spice-wood, red and white mulberry, gensang, Virginia and Seneka snake-root, angelica, sweet-anise, ginger, and wild-hops. The glades are covered with clover, wild-rye, buffalo-grass, and peavine. On the hills, at the heads of rivers, we find stately red-cedars; many of these trees are four feet in diameter, and forty feet clear of limbs. In those hills there is abundance of iron-ore, lead-ore, and coals. Copperas and alumsit for use have been gathered in caves near Nashville.

On the rivers that run into the Mississippi, the growth is nearly the same as on the waters of Cumberland river.

In speaking of a new country, that is extremely fertile and well covered with herbage, it can hardly be necessary to say that it abounds in wild game. The buffalo, elk, deer, and bear, are numerous, nor is there any scarcity of wolves, panthers, wild-cats, foxes, beavers, and otters. They have pheasants, partridges or quails, and turkies in abundance through the year. During the winter, their waters are covered with the swan, wild-goose, brant, and duck. Catfish have been caught in those rivers, that weighed above 100 pounds, and perch that weighed above 20 pounds. Nature seems to measure her works on a different scale on the opposite sides of the Apallachian mountains.

In the year 1780, a small colony under the direction of James Robertson, crossed the mountain, and settled on Cumberland river, at the place now called Nashville. In the year 1783, the state of North-Carolina laid off a tract of land to be reserved for the discharge of military bounties; this reservation included the infant colony, a small tract having been allotted to each of the settlers. A county was also laid off on those waters, called Davidson, to commemorate a brave and popular officer who fell in the service of his country. The bounty lands were run off by surveyors appointed for that purpose; and in a few years a considerable number of the original grantees sold their titles to other persons, and the settlement has lately been increasing very fast. There were 7000 people on that river in September 1791, and their number, since that time, is much increased. We frequently hear of emigrants from the parent state 2 or 300 at a time crossing the mountain.

Of the Soil.

THE farmers on Cumberland river, for the sake of describing their lands, distinguish them by first, second, and third quality. Land of the first quality will bear Indian corn or hemp; but it will not bear wheat without great reduction. Land of the second quality does not bear wheat to advantage until it has been reduced by two or three crops of corn, hemp, tobacco, or cotton. Land of the third quality bears every kind of grain, that is usually sown on dry ground, in the Atlantic states. It is agreed by all who have visited the Cumberland settlement, that 100 bushels of Indian corn are frequently gathered from an acre of their best land. Sixty or seventy bushels from an acre is very common; but the farmer who expects to gather such a crop must be careful, while the corn is soft, to guard it against bears and racoons. This, however, is a trouble that must cease when the country is well settled. Wheat, barley, oats, rye, buckwheat, Indian corn, pease, beans, potatoes of both sorts, flax, hemp, tobacco, indigo, rice, and cotton, have already been planted in that settlement, and they all thrive in great perfection. The usual crop of cotton is 800 pounds to the acre; the staple is long and fine. It is alleged, however, that the lands on the small rivers that run into the Mississippi, have a decided preference to those on the Cumberland river, for the production of cotton and indigo. No experiments have been made on land near the Mississippi, within the ceded territory; but there is a small settlement further down the river, within the limits of the United States, on a similar soil, where the growth and quality of cotton is so remarkable, that its culture is more profitable than any other crop. The soil on those rivers is deep and light, having a small mixture of sand with a black earth; hence, as the planters allege, it proves favourable to the culture of all kinds of roots, as well as of indigo and cotton.

Of the Climate.

THE climate in this country is very temperate; and the experience of ten years assures us, that it is healthy. The piercing northerly winds that prevail, during the winter, in the Atlantic states, seldom molest the inhabitants on Cumberland river, for they have no great mountains to the north or the westward. The inhabitants of the Atlantic states are also subjected to sudden changes in the atmosphere, arising from their vicinity to the ocean; the air that comes from the surface of the sea, especially from the warm Gulf-stream in winter, must be very different in its temperature from the air that comes across cold and high mountains; but the great distance between the Cumberland settlers and the ocean, considering that many great mountains are interposed, effectually secures them against the bad effects of those sudden changes. North-easterly storms never reach this country.

OTHER circumstances present themselves, by which we may account for the remarkable healthiness of this settlement. Lime-stone is common on both sides of Cumberland mountain. The bottom of a river on the west side of the mountain, is frequently a continued stratum of this rock. It is generally known that small streams of water are apt to disappear in countries that abound in lime-stone: this is occasioned, doubtless, by the great fissures that are common in those rocks; from the same cause it probably arises, that we seldom find marshes or stagnant waters where there is much lime-stone. In this territory we find no stagnant waters; and this is certainly one of the reasons why the inhabitants are not afflicted with those bilious and intermitting fevers, which are so frequent, and often fatal, in the same latitude near the coast in Carolina. Whether it proceeds from the goodness of the water, the purity of the air, the temperature of the climate, or whatever else may have been the cause, the inhabitants of that country have certainly been remarkably healthy, ever since they settled on the waters of Cumberland river, whence it appears that the climate is healthy and pleasant.

MEN frequently change their habitations in quest of a better place; and the man, who can enjoy the greatest degree of health, ease, and plenty, is generally supposed to have the most desirable habitation. Keeping this remark in view, perhaps there are few places that present fairer prospects to the man who is looking for a settlement. Few places are more healthy; there is none more fertile; and there is hardly any other place, in which the farmer can support his family in such a degree of affluence. The soil is not only fertile, but easily cultivated. Six hogsheads of tobacco for one man does not require more labour, than three hogsheads in the Atlantic states; and a difference similar to this appears in every other crop. In the culture of corn, the difference is greater. This circumstance alone would secure abundance to the industrious man; but we must also recollect, that, in cold climates, the farmer is shut up or prevented from working several months in the year, during which cold season he is consuming his stores, and his cattle are making greater destruction. When we consider the quantity of food that must be laid up for the necessary support of stock in cold climates, we may fairly calculate, that half of the farmer's time is spent in making provision for his cattle, or in sheltering himself from the weather. In the southern territory, cattle at present support themselves among the reeds, pea-vines, rye-grass, and clover; but when the progress of cultivation shall have destroyed the wild range, it is obvious, that the fodder and straw obtained from the ordinary crops, will be more than sufficient to support the cattle.

LET us review this account. It is granted, that, in cold climates, more than half of the farmer's time is lost from labour by intemperate weather, or taken up in working for the support of his cattle; this gives an odds of two to one in favour of the country that has been described. We are next to recollect, that one day's labour, in this country, produces more than twice as much grain, or other provisions, as it produces in common land, and in a northern climate; this gives another difference of two to one, which makes four to one throughout the year. But, considering that industry, in all countries, bears some proportion to the necessities of the inhabitants, we shall suppose, that the farmer, in this territory, during the year, raises only twice as much provision for his family, as he could raise on common land in

a colder climate; and the difference, as it respects himself, must be immense. In this country, he would live in great affluence, or become rich, by that measure of industry, which, in the other situation, would hardly be sufficient to the support of a miserable life.

PEOPLE, however, are seldom contented with the mere necessaries of life. There are certain luxuries, which the progress of society has taught us to consider as necessary. Sugar, coffee, and tea belong to this class; as do sundry articles of foreign dress. What is the farmer to sell in the western part of the Tennassee government, that he may be enabled to buy foreign articles? He lives at a great distance from sea; how is he to be provided with salt?

IT is very remarkable, that the farmer has more use for salt in the western country, than in the Atlantic states. His cattle, in that country, will not thrive without salt; and this is the only thing, at present, he has occasion to give them. It has already been observed, that lime-stone abounds in the western country; this stone is not found in the southern states, until we approach the first ridge of mountains. As we travel westward, we find lead ore and salt springs in abundance. Does this country abound in articles that are seldom found in the Atlantic states, because it is composed of the original mother earth; whereas the land near the coast, in the middle and southern states, is adventitious? Be this as it may, the salt-springs that are found in every part of the western country, afford the utmost relief to the inhabitants, whose cattle, from the quality of their food, have more need of salt than those who are nearer the sea. Hitherto the salt-works have not been judiciously managed, either at Kentucky or the Cumberland settlement; and yet salt, made from the water of salt-springs, may be purchased for one dollar the bushel. As the source can never fail, and the mode of preparing it is capable of great improvement, we may reasonably suppose, that the average price of salt made on Cumberland river, will be three fourths of a dollar the bushel.

The settlers have not had much experience of bringing loaded boats up the Mississippi; but they calculate, from the trips they have made, that salt may be freighted from New-Orleans to Nashville, at rather less than three eighths of a dollar the bushel; and it appears from similar experiments, that pork, flour, or other produce, may be taken from Nashville to New Orleans at less than three eighths of a dollar the bushel. Those calculations regard the river Mississippi in its present state, with all its circular bendings, the banks covered with trees, and no part of the upper country settled; but the river, at present, is more than double the necessary length. From the mouth of the river Ohio to New-Orleans, the present distance by water is supposed to be 1000 miles; the direct distance is considerably short of 500 miles. In navigating that river we often find places like a horseshoe, where we do not gain more than a mile by sailing or rowing five miles. Every one of those bends may be cut off at a small expense. Let a common ditch, three or four feet deep, be dug across those necks of land, the roots being cut away when the river is low, and the next flood, by the rapidity of the stream through the short passage, will change the ditch to a navigable channel. An experiment of this kind has been made with success, at a place called Point Coupe. Two great benefits will arise from this process of giving the river a straight course; one half of the time and labour in ascending the river, will be saved by shortening the distance. This case supposes that vessels ascend the river by the help of oars, and poles, without sails, which is generally the case at present, because the river is so crooked, that no wind can be fair; but in case the chief bendings of the river should be cut off, as a southerly wind prevails there for the greater part of the year, every vessel would ascend by the use of sails, and the difficulties of that navigation would be reduced to a trifle. Considering what would be the utmost expense of transporting salt from New-Orleans to Nashville, and considering that Nashville is 2 or 300 miles by water farther from New-Orleans, than some other parts of the territory, and presuming that a great share of the present expense may be saved by practicable improvements in the navigation of the Mississippi, we may readily conclude, that the mere freight of the luxuries of life must be a small object to the inhabitants of that territory. As matters are now circumstanced, provided the navigation of the Mississippi was free, the setters on Cumberland river would take their produce to a shipping port, at less expense than it can be waggoned fifty miles in any country.

As the country that has been described, is capable of producing, in great perfection, every article that grows in the Atlantic states, there are no leading circumstances, by which we can possibly determine, what is like to be the general course of its trade, or the particular articles in which its most valuable exports will consist. Iron, lead, pot-ash, pork, bacon, butter, cheese, corn, wheat, barley, flax, hemp, rice, indigo, and cotton, have all been mentioned by different persons from that country, as articles of export. Each of those articles will doubtless be exported in greater or less quantity, according to the demand; but it appears most probable, that the inhabitants will make their chief remittances in tobacco, hemp, rice, indigo, and cotton. The low grounds on the Mississippi must produce great crops of rice, and it has already been observed, that the high grounds near that river are particularly favourable to the culture of indigo and cotton. The article last mentioned must be a constant source of wealth to the planter, because its value is considerable when compared with its weight, and it must be in constant demand in foreign markets. It is hardly necessary to observe, that in a country where timber of the best and most durable quality, and all other materials abound, necessary for shipping, the inhabitants will doubtless build ships for a distant market.

EVERY thing that has been said concerning the advantages to be expected by people who settle in the Tennassee government, is founded on a supposition that all the country may be settled, and the inhabitants permitted to navigate the Mississippi. At present they are greatly restrained on both those heads; but there does not seem to be any violence offered to common sense, nor any great departure from probability, in supposing that the case will be materially altered within a few years. It is hardly worth while to observe, that the navigation of the Mississippi is ours by the express words of treaties; because paper promises are seldom very binding on nations, unless they are supported by other arguments; but it happens in the present case, that arguments more conclusive than treaties present themselves to every attentive mind. Necessity is invincible, and a nation so well informed as the Spaniards must discover, that our fellow citizens on the western waters cannon remain quiet without the use of the Mississippi. The progress of population in that country is no more to be prevented or restrained than the flowing of the rivers. It cannot be retarded by laws, nor by treaties, nor by a stronger curb—the fear of death. The proofs are recent and clear. There was not a single family settled in Kentucky before the year 1775, and the first colony migrated to that country in the face of numerous and hostile savages, when they were more openly supported than of late years, by the British. It is known, that they have continued, from the beginning, in a constant state of war; and yet the settlement, at this hour, contains near one hundred thousand inhabitants. The first adventurers were men, and the increase for several years was chiefly occasioned by emigrants; but women are now become numerous, and the settlement begins to enjoy the benefit of a rapid increase from early marriage and constant emigration. This observation is also applicable to the settlers in the Tennassee government; wherefore, it is a very moderate computation, that supposes four hundred thousand settlers on the western waters by the end of twenty years from this time. Are the inhabitants of such a country to be restrained from going to sea by means of a river that washes their land? Is the little colony of New-Orleans, by the help of a few soldiers, to sustain the weight of such a people, and prevent them from descending? We could as readily believe with the poets, that Mount Atlas sustains the heavens. To say that they are citizens, and must be restrained by the laws of the Union, is to suppose that men will submit to the dominion of laws that are destructive of property—that they will endure oppression, when they can emancipate themselves; that they will suffer under the want of common necessaries, when they have comfortable supplies and riches before their eyes; a case that is not like to happen in America. There are people of such a stamp in the world, but this race does not thrive in the Atlantic states; much less can such a race of animated machines be expected to grow in the western country. Viewing the subject in this point of light, and considering the natural effect of this most unnatural obstruction, events that are very unpleasing present themselves to the mind.

THE western people consider the navigation of the Mississippi as the light of the sun, a birth-right that cannot be alienated. They believe that the national government is bound to support this claim. Let them be told, that their claims, for certain political reasons, cannot be admitted, and they will discover no strength in the argument. They will think of taking by force, the thing that seems to be retained by finesse. Let them be told, that such conduct would be treasonable, and they will reply, that obedience and protection are mutual. If those people should commit a single act of violence on that head, they could not afterwards be restrained by all the powers of the national government. It is true, that the capture of New-Orleans and every post on the Mississippi, would not secure them the navigation of that river. A single frigate at the mouth of the river, would blast the mercantile schemes of all the people in the western country; but we know, that men who have once dipped their feet in treason, are apt to proceed. The penalty is alike for little and for much. Hardy, adventurous men, who are prevented from cultivating the soil, because they are not suffered to carry their produce to sea, may look for some other employment; they may think of a more easy way of getting money. Objects of ambition will not fail to present themselves. Considering, therefore, that the settlement of the western country cannot possibly be retarded; that no human eloquence can dissuade those people from claiming the Mississippi, which is their chief avenue to wealth; that the commerce of Spain might be greatly increased by permitting them to enjoy the free use of that river, and that consequences, unpleasing to both nations, must infallibly arise, from a perseverance in shutting up the river; we may consider the free navigation of the Mississippi as a certain event. By tracing the short lines which mark the Indian boundary, we discover, that all the lands on Duck river and Elk river, as well as on the several rivers which run into the Mississippi, continue to be claimed by the Indians; and those lands are among the best in that country. It may be observed, at the same time, that all those lands are claimed by the Chickasaws, a small tribe of friendly Indians. We may be assured, that the government of the United States will not permit those lands to be settled, without the consent of the Indians; but we must discover, that the natural progress of things, in a short time, will render a considerable part of that country, especially the lands on the Mississippi, useless to the Indians, and necessary to the Whites. Numerous boatmen, passing up and down the river, will have frequent occasion to go on shore; they will need refreshments. Many who go down on rafts or boats, will return by land; they will destroy the game. In a word, every man who lives on the western waters must be interested in having settlements on the Mississippi. There can be little difficulty in making a bargain for a country that is of great use to the Whites, and little use to the Indians. The true interest of the United States would point out a price for those lands, that would enable the Chickasaws to live in a degree of ease and affluence, which otherwise they can never expect. Suppose the Indians should cede all the lands to the northward of Wolf river; in that case, the amount of the North-Carolina grants being deducted, the United States will have at least six millions of acres of good land for sale; lands of such a quality, and so near the sea, will hardly be sold, even by the public, for less than one third of a dollar the acre. Six millions of acres at one third of a dollar, would bring two millions of dollars, by which a debt to that amount must be extinguished, and 120,000 dollars per annum saved to the national treasury. Suppose the twelfth part of the money thus saved, ten thousand dollars, was paid annually to the Chickasaws; one half, in corn or other provisions at a stipulated price; and the other half in clothing; is it not obvious, that their condition would be greatly mended, and equally clear, that the state of our finances would be much improved by such a regulation? It is true, that Indian lands have commonly been obtained on terms much less profitable to the Indians, and more expensive to the Whites; but it may be presumed, that experience will teach us to forsake the old plan, since it is neither recommended by the dictates of humanity nor the rules of economy.

Such is the territory south of the Ohio. The eastern division, as we have observed, is composed of small mountains and vallies, which are extended in the direction of the rivers. There is no plain, or tract of arable land, of any considerable width, in that settlement; but the vallies are generally fertile. In the great western division, there is not a single eminence or ridge, that claims the name of a mountain. This country, nevertheless, is sufficiently diversified by rising ground, and bears no resemblance to the continued plain, which is found near the coast, in the middle and southern states. The rich lands near Cumberland river are considerably broken by knobs or short hills; but those hills have lime-stone for their basis, and are fertile and fit for cultivation to the very top. Streams that run in opposite directions are uniformly divided by rising ground, and some of the ridges are considerably elevated; but they are generally covered with good soil, and are seldom too steep for the plough. There are two remarkable ridges or broken tracks, in that country of considerable dimensions, which are not included in the above description; for they are stony or barren in many places. The first of those ridges divides the waters of Cumberland river from those of the Tennassee; it is broad as it approaches the foot of Cumberland mountain, or rather, diversified in that part by alternate hills and plains; but the plains, being chiefly without timber, are called barrens. The second remarkable tract of broken or barren land, begins near the mouth of Tennessee, dividing the waters of that river from those of the Mississippi, and extending southerly towards the Chickasaw towns. The small rivers that run into the Mississippi, have their heads in this ridge. It is, in some parts, above twenty miles broad, rising at the very margin of the Tennassee. It is covered with long grass, having little or no timber, except a small growth on the water-courses, which are numerous.

The territory west of Cumberland mountain has been stated at fifteen millions of acres; but this calculation leaves eight millions for the Holston settlement, which is certainly too much. The amount that may remain for sale on that side of the mountain, has, in round numbers, been stated at six millions; but the quantity, in all probability, will be considerably greater, without including the great tract of vacant land south of the French Broad, nor the considerable tracts of arable land that are found in

Cumberland mountain, nor those in the Cumberland barrens, so called, where the land, though without timber, is frequently very good; the Indians formerly, in burning the long grass, must have destroyed the trees.

It is probable, that all the lands to the northward of the great bend of the Tennassee, may hereafter be joined to those ceded by North-Carolina, so as to form one state; such a state would have a natural boundary. And when we consider that the Creeks and Chactaws live to the southward, who are numerous nations, together with the Chickasaws, we shall be apt to mark the latitude of the south bend, for a long series of years, as our southern boundary for the purpose of settlement.

The reader has been informed, that the soil, climate, and productions of the country on the western waters, are different from those in the Atlantic states; and it has been intimated, that the whole face of nature in that country bears a different appearance. Observations concerning things that are new or uncommon, should be made and received with caution; but the reader cannot fail to realize the narrative, if he takes the trouble of recollecting two or three remarkable facts, to which reference has already been had.

In the Atlantic states, the strata of lime-stone are

broken, and inclined considerably to the horizon, being, at a medium, nearly parallel to the axis of the earth. In the western country, the strata are constantly found parallel to the horizon.

IN the Atlantic states, salt springs are seldom or never found. In the western country, they abound in every part.

IN the Atlantic states, pit-coal is very scarce, and is obtained with difficulty. In the western country, it is common, and frequently appears within a few feet of the surface.

ONE of those countries must have suffered prodigious convulsions; the other may be supposed to retain more of its original form. Is it at all surprising, that a country, so different in its structure, its appearance, and essential qualities, should produce more plentiful crops, or that it should engage a considerable degree of public attention?

THE END.

THE

CONSTITUTION

OF THE

STATE OF TENNESSEE.

KNOXVILLE,
Printed by GEORGE ROULSTONE, Printer to the State.
1796.

THE

CONSTITUTION

OF THE

STATE OF TENNESSEE.

KNOXVILLE,

Printed by George Roulstone, Printer to the State.

1796.

WE, the People of the Territory of the United States south of the river Ohio, having the right of admission into the general government as a member state thereof, consistent with the Constitution of the United States, and the act of cession of the state of North Carolina, recognizing the ordinance for the government of the Territory of the United States north west of the river Ohio, do ordain and establish the following constitution, or form of government: and do mutually agree with each other to form ourselves into a free and independent state, by the name of THE STATE OF TENNESSEE.

CONSTITUTION, &c.

ARTICLE I.

Section I.

THE legislative authority of this state, shall be vested in a general assembly, which shall consist of a senate and house of representatives, both dependent on the people.

SEC. 2. Within three years after the first meeting of the general assembly, and within every subsequent term of seven years, an enumeration of the taxable inhabitants shall be made in such manner as shall be directed by law; the number of representatives shall, at the several periods of making such enumeration, be fixed by the legislature, and apportioned among the several counties, according to the number of taxable inhabitants in each; and shall never be less than twenty two, nor greater than twenty-six, until the number of taxable inhabitants shall be forty thousand; and after that event, at such ratio that the whole number of representatives shall never exceed forty.

SEC. 3. The number of senators shall, at the several periods of making the enumeration before mentioned, be fixed by the legislature, and apportioned among the districts, formed as herein after directed, according to the number of taxable inhabitants in each, and shall never be less than one third, nor more than one half of the number of representatives.

SEC. 4. The senators shall be chosen by districts, to be formed by the legislature, each district containing such a number of taxable inhabitants, as shall be entitled to elect not more than three senators. When a district shall be composed of two or more counties, they shall be adjoining, and no county shall be divided in forming a district.

SEC. 5. The first election for senators and representatives, shall commence on the second Thursday of March next, and shall continue for that, and the succeeding day; and the next election shall commence on the first Thursday of August, one thousand seven hundred and ninety seven, and shall continue on that and the succeeding day; and forever after, elections shall be held once in two years, commencing on the first Thursday in August, and terminating the succeeding day.

Sec. 6. The first session of the general assembly shall commence on the last Monday of March next. The second on the third Monday of September, one thousand seven hundred and ninety seven. And forever after, the general assembly shall meet on the third Monday of September next ensuing the then election, and at no other period, unless as provided for by this constitution.

Sec. 7. That no person shall be eligible to a seat in the general assembly unless he shall have resided three years in the state, and one year in the county immediately preceding the election, and shall possess in his own right in the county which he represents, not less than two hundred acres of land, and shall have attained to the age of twenty one years.

Sec. 8. The senate and house of representatives, when assembled, shall each choose a speaker and its other officers, be judges of the qualifications and elections of its members, and sit upon its own adjournments from day to day. Two thirds of each house shall constitute a quorum to do business; but a smaller number may adjourn from day to day, and may be authorised, by law, to compel the attendance of absent members.

SEC. 9. Each house may determine the rules of its proceedings, punish its members for disorderly behaviour, and with the concurrence of two thirds, expel a member, but not a second time for the same offence, and shall have all other powers necessary for the legislature of a free state.

SEC. 10. Senators and representatives, shall in all cases, except treason, felony, or breach of the peace, be privileged from arrest during the session of the general assembly, and in going to and returning from the same; and for any speech or debate in either house, they shall not be questioned in any other place.

SEC. 11. Each house may punish, by imprisonment, during their session, any person, not a member, who shall be guilty of disrespect to the house, by any disorderly or contemptuous behaviour in their presence.

SEC. 12. When vacancies happen in either house, the governor, for the time being, shall issue writs of election to fill such vacancies.

SEC. 13. Neither house shall, during their session, adjourn without consent of the other, for more than three days, nor to any other place than that in which the two houses shall be sitting.

Sec. 14. Bills may originate in either house, but may be amended, altered, or rejected by the other.

Sec. 15. Every bill shall be read three times, on three different days, in each house, and be signed by the respective speakers before it becomes a law.

Sec. 16. After a bill has been rejected, no bill containing the same substance, shall be passed into a law during the same session.

Sec. 17. The style of the laws of this state, shall be, Be it enacted by the General Assembly of the State of Tennessee.

Sec. 18. Each house shall keep a journal of its proceedings, and publish them, except such parts as the welfare of the state may require to be kept secret. And the *yeas* and *nays* of the members on any question, shall, at the request of any two of them, be entered on the journals.

Sec. 19. The doors of each house, and committees of the whole, shall be kept open, unless when the business shall be such as ought to be kept secret.

Sec. 20. The legislature of this state shall not allow the following officers of government greater annual salaries than as follows, until the year one thousand eight hundred and four, *to wit.*

The governor not more than seven hundred and fifty dollars.

The judges of the superior courts, not more than six hundred dollars each.

The secretary not more than four hundred dollars.

The treasurer or treasurers, not more than *four per cent.* for receiving and paying out all monies.

The attorney or attornies for the state shall receive a compensation for their services, not exceeding fifty dollars for each superior court which he shall attend.

No member of the legislature shall receive more than one dollar and seventy five cents per day, nor more for every twenty-five miles he shall travel in going to and returning from the general assembly.

SEC. 21. No money shall be drawn from the treasury, but in consequence of appropriations made by law.

SEC. 22. No person who heretofore hath been, or hereafter may be a collector or holder of public monies, shall have a seat in either house of the general assembly, until such person shall have accounted for, and paid into the treasury, all sums for which he may be accountable or liable.

Sec. 23. No judge of any court of law or equity, secretary of state, attorney general, register, clerk of any court of record, or person holding any office under the authority of the United States shall have a seat in the general assembly; nor shall any person, in this state, hold more than one lucrative office at one and the same time; provided, that no appointment in the militia or to the office of a justice of the peace, shall be considered as a lucrative office.

Sec. 24. No member of the general assembly shall be eligible to any office or place of trust, except to the office of a justice of the peace, or trustee of any literary institution, where the powers of appointment to such office or place of trust, is vested in their own body.

Sec. 25. Any member of either house of the general assembly, shall have liberty to dissent from, and protest against any act or resolve which he may think injurious to the public, or any individual, and have the reasons of his dissent entered on the journals.

Sec. 26. All lands liable to taxation, in this state held by deed, grant, or entry, shall be taxed equal and uniform, in such manner, that no one hundred acres shall be taxed higher than another, except town lots, which shall not be taxed higher than two hundred acres of land each; no free man, shall be taxed higher than one hundred acres, and no slave higher than two hundred acres on each poll.

Sec. 27. No article manufactured of the produce of this state, shall be taxed otherwise than to pay inspection fees.

ARTICLE II.

Sec. 1. The supreme executive power of this state shall be vested in a governor.

Sec. 2. The governor shall be chosen by the electors of the members of the general assembly, at the times and places where they shall respectively vote for the members thereof. The returns of every election for governor shall be sealed up, and transmitted to the seat of government, by the returning officers, directed to the speaker of the senate, who shall open and publish them in the presence of a majority of the members of each house of the general assembly. The person having the highest number of votes, shall be governor; but if two or more shall be equal, and highest in votes, one of them shall be chosen governor, by joint ballot of both houses of the general assembly. Contested elections for governor, shall be determined by both houses of the general assembly, in such manner as shall be prescribed by law.

Sec. 3. He shall be at least twenty five years of age, and possess a freehold estate of five hundred acres of land, and have been a citizen or inhabitant of this state four years next before his election, unless he shall have been absent on the public business of the United States, or of this state.

Sec. 4. The first governor shall hold his office until the fourth Tuesday of September, one thousand seven hundred and ninety-seven, and until another governor shall be elected and qualified to office; and forever after, the governor shall hold his office for the term of two years, and until another governor shall be elected and qualified; but shall not be eligible more than six years in any term of eight.

Sec. 5. He shall be commander in chief of the army and navy of this state, and of the militia, except when they shall be called into the service of the United States.

Sec. 6. He shall have power to grant reprieves and pardons, after conviction, except in cases of impeachment.

Sec. 7. He shall, at stated times, receive a compensation for his services, which shall not be increased or diminished during the period, for which he shall have been elected.

Sec. 8. He may require information, in writing, from the officers in the executive department, upon any subject relating to the duties of their respective offices.

Sec. 9. He may on extraordinary occasions, convene the general assembly by proclamation, and shall state to them, when assembled, the purpose for which they shall have been convened.

Sec. 10. He shall take care that the laws shall be faithfully executed.

Sec. 11. He shall, from time to time, give to the general assembly information of the state of the government, and recommend to their consideration such measures as he shall judge expedient.

Sec. 12. In case of his death, or resignation, or removal from office, the speaker of the senate shall exercise the office of governor until another governor shall be duly qualified.

Sec. 13. No member of congress, or person holding any office under the United States, or this state, shall execute the office of governor.

Sec. 14. When any officer, the right of whose appointment is by this constitution vested in the general assembly, shall, during the recess, die, or his office by other means become vacant, the governor shall have power to fill up such vacancy by granting a temporary commission, which shall expire at the end of the next session of the legislature.

Sec. 15. There shall be a seal of this state, which shall be kept by the governor, and used by him officially, and shall be called the great seal of the state of Tennessee.

Sec. 16. All grants and commissions shall be in the name and by the authority of the state of Tennessee, be sealed with the state seal, and signed by the governor.

Sec. 17. A secretary of this state shall be appointed and commissioned during the term of four years.———He shall keep a fair register of all the official acts and proceedings of the governor; and shall, when required, lay the same, and all papers, minutes, and vouchers relative thereto, before the general assembly, and shall perform such other duties as shall be enjoined him by law.

ARTICLE III.

Sec. 1. Every freeman of the age of twenty one

years and upwards, possessing a freehold in the county wherein he may vote, and being an inhabitant of this state, and every free man, being an inhabitant of any one county in the state six months immediately preceding the day of election, shall be entitled to vote for members of the general assembly, for the county in which he shall reside.

SEC. 2. Electors shall in all cases, except treason, felony, or breach of the peace, be privileged from arrest during their attendance at elections, and in going to and returning from them.

SEC. 3. All elections shall be by ballot.

ARTICLE IV.

SEC. 1. The house of representatives shall have the sole power of impeachment.

SEC. 2. All impeachments shall be tried by the senate. When sitting for that purpose, the senators shall be upon oath or affirmation.

SEC. 3. No person shall be convicted, without the concurrence of two thirds of the members of the whole house.

SEC. 4. The governor, and all civil officers under this state, shall be liable to impeachment for any misdemeanor in office; but judgment, in such cases, shall not extend further than to removal from office, and disqualification to hold any office of honour, trust, or profit under this state. The party shall, nevertheless, in all cases be liable to indictment, trial, judgment, and punishment, according to law.

ARTICLE V.

Sec. 1. The judicial power of the state shall be vested in such superior and inferior courts of law and equity, as the legislature shall, from time to time, direct and establish.

Sec. 2. The general assembly shall by joint ballot of both houses, appoint judges of the several courts of law and equity, also an attorney or attornies for the state, who shall hold their respective offices during good behaviour.

Sec. 3. The judges of the superior court shall, at stated times, receive a compensation, for their services, to be ascertained by law; but shall not be allowed any fees or perquisites of office, nor shall they hold any other office of trust or profit under this state, or the United States.

Sec. 4. The judges of the superior courts, shall

be justices of oyer and terminer and general goal delivery, throughout the state.

Sec. 5. The judges of the superior and inferior courts shall not charge juries with respect to matters of fact, but may state the testimony and declare the law.

Sec. 6. The judges of the superior courts shall have power, in all civil cases, to issue writs of *certiorari*, to remove any cause, or a transcript thereof, from any inferior court of record into the superior, on sufficent cause supported by oath or affirmation.

Sec. 7. The judges or justices of the inferior courts of law, shall have power, in all civil cases, to issue writs of *certiorari*, to remove any cause, or a transcript thereof, from any inferior jurisdiction into their court, on sufficient cause, supported by oath or affirmation.

Sec. 8. No judge shall sit on the trial of any cause where the parties shall be connected with him, by affinity or consanguinity, except by consent of parties. In case all the judges of the superior court shall be interested in the event of any cause, or related to all or either of the parties, the governor of the state shall in such case specially commission three men, of law knowledge, for the determination thereof.

Sec. 9. All writs and other process, shall run, IN THE NAME OF THE STATE OF TENNESSEE; and bear test, and be signed by the respective clerks. Indictments shall conclude, AGAINST THE PEACE AND DIGNITY OF THE STATE.

Sec. 10. Each court shall appoint its own clerk, who may hold his office during good behaviour.

Sec. 11. No fine shall be laid on any citizen of this state, that shall exceed fifty dollars, unless it shall be assessed by a jury of his peers, who shall assess the fine at the time they find the fact, if they think the fine ought to be more than fifty dollars.

Sec. 12. There shall be justices of the peace appointed for each county, not exceeding two for each captain's company, except for the company which includes the county town, which shall not exceed three, who shall hold their offices during good behaviour.

ARTICLE VI.

Sec. 1. There shall be appointed in each county, by the county court, one sheriff, one coroner, one trustee, and a sufficient number of constables, who shall hold their offices for two years. They shall also have power to appoint one register and ranger for the county, who shall hold their offices during good behaviour. The sheriff and coroner shall be commissioned by the governor.

SEC. 2. There shall be a treasurer or treasurers appointed for the state, who shall hold his or their offices for two years.

SEC. 3. The appointment of all officers not otherwise directed by this constitution, shall be vested in the legislature.

ARTICLE VII.

SEC. 1. Captains, subalterns, and non commissioned officers, shall be elected by those citizens, in their respective districts, who are subject to military duty.

SEC. 2. All field officers of the militia shall be elected by those citizens in their respective counties who are subject to military duty.

SEC. 3. Brigadiers general shall be elected by the field officer of their respective brigades.

SEC. 4. Majors general shall be elected by the brigadiers and field officers of the respective divisions.

SEC. 5. The governor shall appoint the adjutant general; the majors general shall appoint their aids;

the brigadiers general shall appoint their brigade majors; and the commanding officers of regiments their adjutants and quarter masters.

Sec. 6. The captains and the subalterns of the cavalry shall be appointed by the troops enrolled in their respective companies, and the field officers of the district shall be appointed by the said captains and subalterns, provided, that whenever any new county is laid off, that the field officers of the said cavalry shall appoint the captain and other officers therein, *pro tempore*, until the company is filled up and completed, at which time the election of the captains and subalterns shall take place as aforesaid.

Sec. 7. The legislature shall pass laws, exempting citizens belonging to any sect or denomination of religion, the tenets of which are known to be opposed to the bearing of arms, from attending private and general musters.

ARTICLE VIII.

Sec. 1. Whereas the ministers of the gospel are, by their professions, dedicated to God and the care of souls, and ought not to be diverted from the great duties of their functions; therefore no minister of the gospel, or priest of any denomination whatever, shall be eligible to a seat in either house of the legislature.

Sec. 2. No person who denies *the being of God, or a future state of rewards and punishments*, shall hold any office in the civil department of this state.

ARTICLE IX.

Sec. 1. That every person, who shall be chosen or appointed to any office of trust or profit, shall, before entering on the execution thereof, take an oath to support the constitution of this state, and also an oath of office.

Sec. 2. That each member of the senate and house of representatives, shall, before they proceed to business, take an oath or affirmation to support the constitution of this state, and also the following oath:

I, A. B. do solemnly swear (or affirm) that, as a member of this general assembly, I will in all appointments vote without favor, affection, partiality, or prejudice, and that I will not propose or assent to any bill, vote, or resolution which shall appear to me injurious to the people, or consent to any act or thing whatever, that shall have a tendancy to lessen or abridge their rights and privileges, as declared by the constitution of this state.

SEC. 3. Any elector who shall receive any gift or reward for his vote, in *meat*, *drink*, *money*, or otherwise, shall suffer such punishment as the laws shall direct. And any person who shall directly or indirectly give, promise, or bestow any such reward to be elected, shall thereby be rendered incapable, for two years, to serve in the office for which he was elected, and be subject to such further punishment as the legislature shall direct.

SEC. 4. No new county shall be established by the general assembly, which shall reduce the county or counties, or either of them, from which it shall be taken, to a less content than six hundred and twenty five square miles. Nor shall any new county be laid off, of less contents. All new counties, as to the right of suffrage and representation, shall be considered as a part of the county or counties from which it was taken, until entitled by numbers to the right of representation. No bill shall be passed into a law, for the establishment of a new county, except upon a petition to the general assembly, for that purpose, signed by two hundred of the free male inhabitants within the limits or bounds of such new county prayed to be laid off.

ARTICLE X.

Sec. 1. Knoxville shall be the seat of government, until the year one thousand eight hundred and two.

Sec. 2. All laws and ordinances now in force and use in this territory, not inconsistent with this constitution, shall continue to be in force and use in this state, until they shall expire, be altered, or repealed by the legislature.

Sec. 3. That whenever two thirds of the general assembly shall think it necessary to amend or change this constitution, they shall recommend to the electors, at the next election for members to the general assembly, to vote for or against a convention; and if it shall appear that a majority of all the citizens of the state, voting for representatives, have voted for a convention, the general assembly shall, at their next session, call a convention, to consist of as many members as there be in the general assembly, to be chosen in the same manner, at the same place, and by the same electors, that chose the general assembly, who shall meet within three months after the said election, for the purpose of revising, amending or changing the constitution.

Sec. 4. The declaration of rights hereto annexed, is declared to be a part of the constitution of this state, and shall never be violated on any pretence whatever. And to guard against transgressions of the high powers which we have delegated, we declare, that every thing in the bill of rights contained, and every other right not hereby delegated, is excepted out of the general powers of government, and shall forever remain inviolate.

ARTICLE XI.

DECLARATION OF RIGHTS.

I. That all power is inherent in the people, and all free governments are founded on their authority, and instituted for their peace, safety, and happiness: for the advancement of those ends, they have at all times an unalienable and indefeasible right to alter, reform, or abolish the government in such manner as they may think proper.

II. That government being instituted for the common benefit, the doctrine of non resistance against arbitrary power and oppression is absurd, slavish, and destructive to the good and happiness of mankind.

III. That all men have a natural and indefeasible right to worship Almighty God according to the dictates of their own consciences; that no man can of right be compelled to attend, erect, or support any place of worship, or to maintain any ministry against his consent; that no human authority can in any case whatever controul or interfere with the rights of conscience; and that no preference shall ever be given by law to any religious establishments or modes of worship.

IV. That no religious test shall ever be required as a qualification to any office or public trust under this state.

V. That elections shall be free and equal.

VI. That the right of trial by jury shall remain inviolate.

VII. That the people shall be secure in their persons, houses, papers, and possessions, from unreasonable searches, and seizures, and that general warrants, whereby an officer may be commanded to search suspected places, without evidence of the fact committed, or to seize any person or persons not named, whose offences are not particularly described and supported by evidence, are dangerous to liberty, and ought not to be granted.

VIII. That no freeman shall be taken, or imprisoned, or disseized of his freehold, liberties, or privileges, or outlawed, or exiled, or in any manner destroyed, or deprived of his life, liberty, or property but by the judgment of his peers, or the law of the land.

IX. That in all criminal prosecutions, the accused hath a right to be heard by himself, and his counsel, to demand the nature and cause of the accusation against him, and to have a copy thereof; to meet the witnesses face to face; to have compulsory process for obtaining witnesses in his favour; and in prosecutions by indictment, or presentment, a speedy public trial, by an impartial jury of the county or district in which the crime shall have been committed; and shall not be compelled to give evidence against himself.

X. That no person shall, for the same offence, be twice put in jeopardy of life or limb.

XI. That laws made for the punishment of facts committed previous to the existence of such laws, and by them only declared criminal, are contrary to the principles of a free government; wherefore no *ex post facto* law shall be made.

XII. That no conviction shall work corruption of blood or forfeiture of estate.—The estate of such persons as shall destroy their own lives, shall descend or vest as in case of natural death.—If any person be killed by casualty, there shall be no forfeiture in consequence thereof.

XIII. That no person arrested, or confined in goal, shall be treated with unnecessary rigour.

XIV. That no freeman shall be put to answer any criminal charge, but by presentment, indictment, or impeachment.

XV. That all prisoners shall be bailable by sufficient sureties, unless for capital offences, when the proof is evident or the presumption great. And the privilege of the writ of *habeas corpus* shall not be suspended, unless when in case of rebellion or invasion the public safety may require it.

XVI. That excessive bail shall not be required, nor excessive fines imposed, nor cruel and unusual punishments inflicted.

XVII. That all courts shall be open; and every man, for an injury done him in his lands, goods, person, or reputation, shall have remedy by due course of law, and right and justice administered without sale, denial, or delay. Suits may be brought against the state in such manner, and in such courts as the legislature may by law direct, provided the right of bringing suit be limited to the citizens of this state.

XVIII. That the person of a debtor, where there is not strong presumption of fraud, shall not be continued in prison, after delivering up his estate for the benefit of his creditor or creditors, in such manner as shall be prescribed by law.

XIX. That the printing presses shall be free to every person who undertakes to examine the proceedings of the legislature, or of any branch or officer of government; and no law shall ever be made to restrain the right thereof. The free communication of thoughts and opinions, is one of the invaluable rights of man; and every citizen may freely speak, write, and print on any subject, being responsible for the abuse of that liberty. But in prosecutions for the publication of papers investigating the official conduct of officers or men in public capacity, the truth thereof may be given in evidence; and in all indictments for libels, the jury shall have a right to determine the law and the facts, under the direction of the court, as in other cases.

XX. That no retrospective law, or law impairing the obligation of contracts, shall be made.

XXI. That no man's particular services shall be

demanded, or property taken, or applied to public use, without the consent of his representatives, or without just compensation being made therefor.

XXII. That the citizens have a right, in a peaceable manner, to assemble together for their common good, to instruct their representatives, and to apply to those invested with the powers of government for redress of grievances, or other proper purposes, by address or remonstrance.

XXIII. That perpetuities and monopolies are contrary to the genius of a free state, and shall not be allowed.

XXIV. That the sure and certain defence of a free people is a well regulated militia; and as standing armies, in time of peace, are dangerous to freedom, they ought to be avoided, as far as the circumstances and safety of the community will admit; and that in all cases the military shall be in strict subordination to the civil authority.

XXV. That no citizen in this state, except such as are employed in the army of the United States, or militia in actual service, shall be subject to corporeal punishment under the martial law.

XXVI. That the freemen of this state have a

right to keep and to bear arms for their common defence.

XXVII. That no soldier shall, in time of peace, be quartered in any house without consent of the owner, nor in time of war, but in a manner prescribed by law.

XXVIII. That no citizen of this state shall be compelled to bear arms, provided he will pay an equivalent, to be ascertained by law.

XXIX. That an equal participation of the free navigation of the Mississippi, is one of the inherent rights of the citizens of this state: it cannot therefore, be conceded to any prince, potentate, power, person, or persons whatever.

XXX. That no hereditary emoluments, privileges, or honours shall ever be granted or conferred in this state.

XXXI. That the people residing south of French Broad and Holston, between the rivers Tennessee and the Big Pigeon, are entitled to the right of pre-emption and occupancy in that tract.

XXXII. That the limits and boundaries of this state be ascertained, it is declared they are as hereafter mentioned; that is to say:——Beginning on the extreme height of the Stone Mountain, at the place where the line of Virginia intersects it, in latitude thirty six degrees and thirty minutes North—running thence along the extreme height of the said Mountain, to the place where Watauga River breaks through it; thence a direct course to the top of the Yellow Mountain, where Bright's road crosses the same; thence along the ridge of said Mountain, between the waters of Doe River and the waters of Rock Creek, to the place where the road crosses the Iron Mountain; from thence along the extreme height of said Mountain to where Nolichucky River runs through the same; thence to the top of the Bald Mountain: thence along the extreme height of said Mountain to the painted Rock, on French Broad River; thence along the highest ridge of said Mountain, to the place where it is called the Great Iron or Smoky Mountain; thence along the extreme height of said Mountain to the place where it is called Unicoi or Unaka Mountain, between the Indian Towns of Cowee and Old Chota; thence along the main ridge of the said Mountain to the southern boundary of this state, as described in the act of cession of North-Carolina to the United States of America; and that all the Territory lands and waters lying West of the said line, as before mentioned, and contained within the chartered limits of the state of North-Carolina, are within the boundaries and limits of this state, over which the people have the right of exercising sovereignty and right of soil so far as is consistent with the constitution of the United States, recognizing the articles of confederation, the bill of rights and constitution of North Carolina, the cession act of the said state, and the ordinance of the late Congress, for the government of the Territory North-West of the Ohio; provided, nothing herein contained shall extend to affect the claim or claims of individuals, to any part of the soil which is recognized to them by the aforesaid cession act.

SCHEDULE.

Sec. 1. That no inconvenience may arise from a change of the temporary to a permanent state government, it is declared, that all right, actions, prosecutions, claims, and contracts, as well of individuals as of bodies corporate, shall continue, as if no change had taken place in the administration of government.

Sec. 2. All fines, penalties, and forfeitures, due and owing to the territory of the United States of America south of the river Ohio, shall enure to the use of the state. All bonds for performance, executed to the governor of the said territory, shall be and pass over to the governor of this state, and his successors in office, for the use of the state, or by him or them respectively to be assigned over to the use of those concerned, as the case may be.

SEC. 3. The governor, secretary, judges and brigadiers general have a right, by virtue of their appointments, under the authority of the United States, to continue in the exercise of the duties of their respective offices, in their several departments, until the said officers are superseded under the authority of this constitution.

SEC. 4. All officers, civil and military, who have been appointed by the governor, shall continue to exercise their respective offices until the second Monday in June, and until successors in office shall be appointed under the authority of this constitution, and duly qualified.

SEC. 5. The governor shall make use of his private seal, until a state seal shall be provided.

SEC. 6. Until the first enumeration shall be made, as directed in the second section of the first article of this constitution, the several counties shall be respectively entitled to elect one senator and two representatives: Provided that no new county shall be entitled to separate representation previous to taking the enumeration.

Sec. 7. That the next election for representatives and other officers, to be held for the county of Tennessee, shall be held at the house of *William Miles*.

Sec. 8. Until a land office shall be opened, so as to enable the citizens south of French Broad and Holston, between the rivers Tennessee and Big Pigeon, to obtain titles upon their claims of occupancy and pre-emption, those who hold land by virtue of such claims, shall be eligible to serve in all capacities, where a freehold is by this constitution made a requisite qualification.

DONE in convention at Knoxville, by unanimous consent, on the sixth day of February, in the year of our Lord, one thousand seven hundred and ninety six, and of the independence of the United States of America, the twentieth.—In Testimony whereof we have hereunto subscribed our names.

WILLIAM BLOUNT,
PRESIDENT.

BLOUNT COUNTY.
David Craig.
James Greenaway.
Joseph Black.
James Houston.
Samuel Glass.

SULLIVAN COUNTY.
George Rutledge.
William C. C. Claiborne.
Richard Gammon.
John Shelby, jun.
John Rhea.

DAVIDSON COUNTY.
John M'Nairy.
Andrew Jackson.
James Robertson.
Thomas Hardiman.
Joel Lewis.

GREENE COUNTY.
Samuel Frazier.
Stephen Brooks.
William Rankin.
Elisha Baker.
John Galbreath.

HAWKINS COUNTY.
James Berry.
Joseph M'Min.
Thomas Henderson.
William Cocke.
Richard Mitchell.

JEFFERSON COUNTY.
Alexander Outlaw.
Joseph Anderson.
George Doherty.
James Roddye.
Archibald Roane.

KNOX COUNTY.
James White.
Charles M'Clung.
John Crawford.
John Adair.

SUMMER COUNTY.
David Shelby.
Isaac Walton.
W. Douglass.
Edward Douglass.
Daniel Smith.

SEVIER COUNTY.
Peter Bryan.

Samuel Wier.
Spencer Clack.
John Clack.
Thomas Buckenham.

TENNESSEE COUNTY.
Thomas Johnston.
James Ford.
William Fort.
William Prince.
Robert Prince.

WASHINGTON COUNTY.
John Tipton.
Samuel Handly.
Leeroy Taylor.
Landon Carter.
James Stuart.

Attest.

WILLIAM MACLIN, Secretary.

A CATECHETICAL EXPOSITION

OF THE

CONSTITUTION

OF THE

STATE OF TENNESSEE:

Inteaded principally for the use of SCHOOLS.

By WILLIE BLOUNT, Esq.

KNOXVILLE,
PRINTED BY GEORGE ROULSTONE.
1803.

A

CATECHETICAL EXPOSITION

OF THE

CONSTITUTION

OF THE

STATE OF *TENNESSEE:*

Intended principally for the use of SCHOOLS.

By WILLIE BLOUNT, Esq.

KNOXVILLE.

Printed by GEORGE ROULSTONE.

1803.

THE

CONSTITUTION, &c.

Question When did the convention, which formed the constitution of the state of Tennessee meet; where was it holden; when did it adjourn?

Answer It met on the 11th of January at Knoxville, and adjourned the 6th of February, 1796, and of the independence of the United States of America the twentieth.

Q. How many members composed the convention?

A. Fifty five.—Five from each county in the state (then Territory South of Ohio.)

Q. What sum were the members allowed per day?

A. Two dollars and fifty cents was allowed each member per day, and the same to each for every thirty miles travelling to and from the convention —It appears that the above allowance was made, and the sum necessary to defray the expence of the convention, appropriated by the last Territorial Assembly.—It also appears, that the members of the convention allowed themselves less, viz one dollar and fifty cents per day, and one dollar for every thirty miles they travelled to and from the convention.—And it further appears, that the convention unanimously resolved, not to receive the money which had been appropriated to their use, by law, and expressed a wish, that the next assembly would appropriate so much thereof to the payment of the secretary, clerk, printer, and door keeper as would be sufficient to pay them for their services.

Q. Who was president of the convention?

A. William Blount.

Q. Who was secretary, and who was his assistant, and what was their pay per day?

A. William Maclin was secretary, John Sevier, junior, assistant; allowed two dollars and fifty cents each per day.

Q. Who was door keeper, and what was his pay per day?

A. John Rhea, of Blount county—his allowance, two dollars per day.

Q. Who was the printer, and what was his allowance?

A. Geo. Roulstone;—and his allowance was 166 dolls. 66 cents.

Q. What was the whole amount of expence incurred by the convention?

A. 3,007 dolls. 68 cents—and for the reason above mentioned, 455 dolls. 78 cts. only became necessary to be paid.

Q. Who were the members of the convention?

A. From *Davidson county.* John M'Nairy, Andrew Jackson, James Robertson, Thomas Hardeman, and Joel Lewis.

Blount, David Craig, James Greenaway, Joseph Black, Samuel Glass & James Houston.

Greene, Samuel Frazier, Stephen Brooks, Wm. Rankin, Elisha Baker, & John Galbreath.

Hawkins, James Berry, Joseph M'Minn, Thomas Henderson, William Cocke, and Richard Mitchell.

Jefferson, Alexander Outlaw, Joseph Anderson, George Doherty, James Roddye, and Archibald Roane.

Knox, James White, William Blount, Charles M'Clung, John Crawford, and John Adair.

Sullivan, George Rutledge, Wm. C. C. Claiborne, Richard Gammon,

John Shelby, jun. and John Rhea.

Sumner, David Shelby, Isaac Walton, William Douglass, Edward Douglass, and Daniel Smith.

Sevier, Peter Bryan, Samuel Wear, Spencer Clack, John Clack and Thomas Buckingham.

Tennessee, Thomas Johnston, James Ford, Wm. Fort, Wm. Prince, and Robert Prince.

Washington, John Tipton, Samuel Handley, Leeroy Taylor, Landon Carter, and James Stuart.

Q. Did the above named persons all sign the constitution?

A. Yes.

ARTICLE I.

Q. Where is the legislative authority vested?

A. In a General Assembly, consisting of two distinct branches, to wit, Senate and House of Representatives.

Q. On whom are both branches of the legislature dependent for their election?

A. On the Sovereign People.

Q. Within what period was the first enumeration to be made?

A. Within three years after the first meeting of the assembly.

Q. Was it made?

A. Yes.

Q. Within what period is enumerations to be made subsequent to the three years after the first meeting of the assembly?

A. Within every term of seven years, which shall be directed by law, as to the manner of taking it.

Q. Are citizens of all descriptions to be enumerated within every seven years?

A. No—only the taxable inhabitants.

Q. How were the senators and representatives apportioned and elected prior to the first enumeration?

A. One senator and two representatives were elected in each county by the people.

Q. When did the first election for senators and representatives commence?

A. On the second Thursday of March, 1796, and closed the day following.

Q. When did the next election commence?

A. On the first Thursday of August, 1797, and ended on the succeeding day.

Q. When shall future elections for senators and

representatives commence, and how often shall elections be held?

A. They shall be held once in two years, and shall commence on the first Thursday in August, and end the succeeding day.

Q. When did the first session of the assembly commence?

A. On the last Monday in March, 1796.

Q. When did the next assembly commence?

A. On the third Monday of September, 1797.

Q. When shall future assemblies commence?

A. On the third Monday of September next ensuing the then election.

Q. May the assembly meet at no other period?

A. Not unless called by the governor.

Q. How, after the expiration of three years after the first meeting of the Assembly, and after the first enumeration, shall the representatives be apportioned?

A. By the assembly, according to the number of taxable inhabitants in each county, immediately after each enumeration, and so apportion them that the number of representatives shall not be less than twenty two, nor greater than twenty six, until there are 40,000 taxable inhabitants; and after that so as that the whole number of representatives shall never exceed 40.

Q. How are senators apportioned, and what number may there be?

A. By the assembly among the districts, to be formed by the assembly, according to the number of taxable inhabitants in each, immediately after each enumeration, and their number shall never be less than one third, nor more than one half of the number of the representatives.

Q. How are senators to be chosen?

A. By districts to be formed by the assembly immediately after each enumeration.

Q. Shall any district be formed that shall be entitled to elect more than three senators?

A. No.

Q. When a district shall be formed of two, or more counties, shall they be adjoining?

A. Yes.

Q. Can any county be divided in forming a district?

A. No county shall be divided in forming an election district for senators.

Q. What is necessary to constitute a man eligible to a seat in general assembly?

A. To have resided three years in this state, one year in the county, immediately preceding the election, to be twenty one years of age, and shall have possessed, and continue to possess in the county, two hundred acres of land for one year preceding his election.

Q. How many members form a quorum to do business?

A. Two thirds of each house.

Q. Cannot a smaller number do some business?

A. Yes, they may adjourn from day to day, and may be authorized by law to compel the attendance of absent members.

Q. How are the speakers and other officers of the two branches chosen?

A. Each house shall chuse their speaker and other officers, and be judges of the qualifications and elections of its members, and sit upon its own adjournments from day to day.

Q. Can either house punish or expel a member?

A. Yes, either house may punish its members for disorderly behaviour, and with the concurrence of two thirds expel a member; but not a second time for the same offence.

Q. Who shall determine the rules of the proceedings of each house?

A. Each house may determine the rules of its proceedings.

Q. Are all powers necessary for a free state vested in the legislature?

A. Yes.

Q. Are senators and representatives privileged from arrest in all cases during the session, and whilst going to, and returning home from the assembly?

A. Yes, except for treason, felony or breach of the peace.

Q. Can each house punish by imprisonment during the session, any person not a member?

A. Yes, if that person is guilty of disrespect to the house, by any disorderly or contemptuous behaviour in their presence.

Q. When vacancies happen in either house, how are they to be filled?

A. The governor shall issue writs of election.

Q. Shall either house during their session, adjourn without the consent of the other?

A. Not for a longer time than three days.

Q. Can either house during their session, adjourn to any other place than that in which the two houses shall be sitting?

A. No.

Q. May bills originate in either house?

A. Yes; but they may be altered, amended, or rejected by the other.

Q. How often shall a bill be read before it becomes a law?

A. Three times, on three different days in each house, and be signed by the speakers.

Q. If a bill is rejected, shall any bill containing the same substance be passed into a law the same session?

A. No.

Q. What shall be the style of the laws of this state?

A. Be it enacted by the General Assembly of the State of Tennessee.

Q. Shall each house keep a journal of its proceedings?

A. Yes.

Q. Shall they be published?

A. Yes, except such parts as the welfare of the state may require to be kept secret.

Q. Shall the yeas and nays on any question be entered on the journal?

A. Yes, at the request of any two members.

Q. Shall the doors of each house, and committees of the whole, be kept open?

A. Yes, unless when the business shall be such as ought to be kept secret.

Q. Who allows the following named officers of government their annual salaries, and how much may be allowed to each, *to wit*, the governor, judges of the superior court, secretary, treasurers, and attornies for the state?

A. The legislature fix the salaries; but until the

year 1804, they shall not allow greater annual salaries

To the Governor, than seven hundred and fifty dollars,

To the Judges, not more than six hundred dollars,

To the Secretary, not more than four hundred dollars,

To the Treasurer or Treasurers, not more than four per cent for receiving and paying out all monies,

To the Attorney or Attornies, not more than fifty dollars for each superior court he shall attend.

Q. What is the pay of a member of assembly per day, during the session?

A. No member of the assembly shall receive more than one dollar and seventy five cents per day, nor more for every twenty five miles he travels, going to, and returning from the general assembly.

Q. How shall money be drawn from the treasury?

A. Not otherwise than in consequence of appropriations made by law.

Q. Shall any person who has heretofore, or hereafter may be a collector or holder of public money, have a seat in either house?

A. Not until he shall have accounted for, and

paid into the treasury all sums for which he may be accountable or liable.

Q. Shall a judge of any court of law or equity, secretary of state, attorney general, register, clerk of any court of record, or person holding any office under the authority of the United States, have a seat in the assembly; or shall any person in this state hold more than one lucrative office at the same time?

A. No, provided no appointment in the militia, or to the office of justice of the peace, shall be considered a lucrative office.

Q. Shall any member of assembly be eligible to an office or place of trust, where the power of appointment is vested in the assembly?

A. No, except to the office of justice of the peace, or trustee of any literary institution.

Q. Can any member of either house dissent from, and protest against any act or resolve?

A. Yes, if he thinks it either injurious to the public, or to an individual, and have his reasons of dissent entered on the journals.

Q. How are lands taxed?

A. They shall be taxed equal and uniform throughout the state except town lots, where it is liable to taxation.

Q. What lands are liable to taxation?

A. All lands held by deed, grant or entry.

Q. Can a town lot be taxed higher than two hundred acres of land?

A. No.

Q. Do free men pay a poll tax, and how high may they be taxed?

A. Yes, but the tax shall not exceed the tax on one hundred acres of land.

Q. Do the owners of slaves pay any tax on them?

A. Yes, not to exceed the tax on 200 acres of land.

Q. Shall any article manufactured of the produce of this state, be taxed?

A. Not otherwise than to pay the inspection fees.

ARTICLE II.

Q. Where is the executive power of the state vested?

A. In a governor.

Q. How, and when is the governor elected?

A. By the electors of the members of assembly, and at the same time and place that they elect members of assembly.

Q. How are the returns of the votes for governor made?

A. The votes taken in each county are sent to the seat of government by the sheriffs or returning officers, under seal, directed to the speaker of the senate, who shall open and publish them in the presence of a majority of the members of each house.

Q. Is the person highest in votes elected governor, or must he have a majority of the whole number of votes to elect him?

A. The person highest in votes is elected.

Q. Suppose two have an equal number of votes, and they are highest in votes, how shall the election be decided?

A. By joint ballot of both houses.

Q. How shall contested elections for governor to be decided?

A. By both houses, in such a manner as shall be prescribed by law.

Q. What are the requisites to constitute a citizen eligible to the office of governor?

A. He must be twenty five years of age, possessed of a freehold estate of five hundred acres of land, and shall have been a citizen or inhabitant of this state four years next before his election unless he shall have been absent on public business of the United States, or of this state.

Q. For what length of time is the governor elected?

A. For two years, and until a successor shall be elected and qualified.

Q. For what term of years is he eligible?

A. Not more than six, in any term of eight years.

Q. When did writs of election issue for holding the first election of members of assembly to represent the state of Tennessee in general assembly, and for governor, and who was authorized to issue those writs, and to whom were they directed?

A. The president of the convention was by that body authorized to issue writs of election to the sheriffs of the several counties for the above purpose, to bear date February 6th, 1796.

Q. How long did the first Governor of Tennessee hold his office under his first election?

A. From the 30th March 1796 the day he was qualified into office, until the 4th Tuesday of September 1797, and until another was elected and qualified.

Q. Who is commander in chief of the militia army and navy of this state?

A. The governor, except when the militia are called into the service of the United States.

Q. Who is empowered to grant reprieves and pardons?

A. The governor after conviction.

Q. Has he power to grant them in cases of impeachment?

A. No.

Q. Can the governor's salary be increased or diminished, during the term for which he was elected?

A. No.

Q. May the governor require information in writing, from the officers in the executive department?

A. Yes, upon any subject respecting the duties of their respective offices.

Q. May the governor convene the legislature?

A. Yes, upon extraordinary occasions.

Q. How shall he convene them?

A. By proclamation.

Q. Is he bound to state in the proclamation, the purpose for which he convenes them?

A. No, but he is obliged to state the purpose to them after they are assembled.

Q. Is it a duty enjoined on the governor to take care that the laws be faithfully executed?

A. Yes.

Q. Shall the governor from time to time, give to the assembly information of the state of the government?

A. Yes.

Q. Is the governor bound to recommend measures to the assembly?

A. Yes, such as he shall judge expedient.

Q. In case of the death, resignation or removal from office of the governor, who shall act as governor?

A. The speaker of the senate, until another governor is duly qualified.

Q. Can a member of congress, an officer under the United States, or of this state, exercise the office of governor?

A. No.

Q. If an officer appointed by the assembly dies, or his office by other means becomes vacant in the recess of the assembly, who is authorized to fill the vacancy?

A. The governor has authority to issue a commission which shall expire at the end of the next session of assembly.

Q. Is it necessary for the state to have a seal?

A. Yes.

Q. Whose duty is it to keep the seal?

A. The governor.

Q. Is the governor bound to affix it to all official acts?

A. Yes.

Q. How shall all grants and commissions run?

A. In the name and by the authority of the state of Tennessee.

Q. Shall they bear the seal of the state, and be signed by the governor?

A. Yes.

Q. What is the duty of the secretary of state, and for what term of years shall he hold his office?

A. He shall keep a fair register of all the official acts and proceedings of the governor; and may hold his office four years.

Q. Can the assembly require the secretary to lay the official acts and proceedings of the governor before them?

A. Yes.

Q. Can the assembly require all such papers, minutes and vouchers relative to those acts and proceedings to be laid before them by the secretary?

A. Yes.

Q. Are no other duties required of the secretary?

A. Yes, he shall perform such other duties as shall be enjoined on him by law.

ARTICLE III.

Q. What are the requisites to entitle a citizen to vote for members of assembly?

A. He must be a free man, 21 years old, be possessed of a freehold in the county where he votes, he must be an inhabitant of this state, or must have resided in some county six months, immediately preceding the day of election, and he may be entitled to vote for members for the county in which he shall reside.

Q. Are electors privileged from arrests in all cases, during their attendance at elections, and in going to and returning from them?

A. They are not; they may be arrested for treason, felony or breach of the peace; but except in these cases they are privileged.

Q. Shall all elections be by ballot?

A. Yes.

ARTICLE IV.

Q. Who shall have the sole power to impeach?

A. The house of representatives.

Q. Who shall try impeachments?

A. The senate.

Q. Shall senators when sitting on the trial of an impeachment be on oath or affirmation?

A. Yes.

Q. What number of senators does it require to convict, on an impeachment?

A. Two thirds of the whole house must concur.

Q. Who are liable to impeachment, and for what?

A. The governor, and all civil officers of the state, for any misdemeanor in office.

Q. How far may judgments on impeachment in cases of conviction extend?

A. To a removal from, and disqualification to the holding any office of honor, profit or trust under this state.

Q. Is the person impeached, in all cases, liable to indictment, trial, judgment and punishment?

A. Yes, according to law.

ARTICLE V.

Q. Where is the judicial power of the state vested?

A. In such superior and inferior courts of law and equity as the legislature from time to time may establish.

Q. By whom, and how are judges of the superior courts of law and equity elected?

A. The assembly elect by joint ballot of both houses.

Q. By whom, and how is the attorney general elected?

A. The assembly by joint ballot of both houses elect—there may be more attornies general than one.

Q. On what tenure do judges and attornies general hold their offices?

A. During good behaviour.

Q. How are they to receive their salaries?

A. At stated times to be ascertained by law.

Q. Can judges receive any fees or perquisites of office?

A. No.

Q. Shall they hold any other office of profit or trust under this state, or the United States?

A. No.

Q. Who shall be justices of oyer and terminer, and general jail delivery throughout the state?

A. The justices of the superior courts.

Q. May judges of the superior and inferior courts, charge juries with respect to matters of fact?

A. They are expressly forbidden.

Q. Shall they state the testimony and declare the law to the jury?

A. Yes, they may do so.

Q. Have the judges of the superior courts power, in all civil cases, to issue writs of *certiorari*, to remove any cause or transcript thereof, from any inferior court of record, into the superior court?

A. Yes, on sufficient cause shown by the party praying it, and supported by oath or affirmation.

Q. Have the judges of the superior courts power to remove by *certiorari*, any cause or transcript thereof, from any inferior jurisdiction, into their court?

A. Yes, in all civil cases, on sufficient cause, supported by oath or affirmation.

Q. Shall a judge sit on the trial of any cause where the parties are connected with him, by affinity or consanguinity?

A. Not unless by consent of parties.

Q. Suppose all the judges of the superior court are interested in the event of a cause, or connected with either party, how is the cause to be tried?

A. The governor shall commission three men of law knowledge for the determination thereof.

Q. How shall all writs and other process run?

A. In the name of the state of Tennessee.

Q. By whom shall all writs and other process be signed and bear test?

A. By the respective clerks.

Q. How shall indictments conclude?

A. Against the peace and dignity of the state.

Q. Who shall appoint clerks of courts?

A. Each court shall appoint its own clerk.

Q. On what tenure do clerks hold their offices?

A. During good behaviour.

Q. To what extent may the judges of the superior, or the justices of the county courts fine a citizen?

A. Not higher than fifty dollars.

Q. Can no citizen be fined higher than fifty dollars?

A. Yes, the jury may at the time they find the fact, assess a higher fine, if they think it ought to exceed fifty dollars, and they shall in such cases, assess it at the time they find the fact.

Q. Shall there be justices of the peace in each county?

A. Yes.

Q. How many may there be in each county?

A. Not exceeding two for each captain's company, except for that company which includes the county town, and it shall not exceed three.

Q. By whom are justices appointed?

A. They are nominated by both houses of assembly, and commissioned by the governor.

Q. On what tenure do they hold their appointments?

A. During good behaviour.

ARTICLE VI.

Q. How many sheriffs, coroners, county trustees, and constables, shall there be in each county, and how shall they be appointed?

A. There shall be appointed by the county courts, one sheriff, one coroner, one trustee, and a sufficient number of constables in each county.

Q. How long may sheriffs, coroners, trustees, and constables, hold office?

A. Two years, but are again eligible.

Q. How are registers and rangers appointed, and how many may there be in each county?

A. The county court shall appoint one register, and one ranger in each county.

Q. How long shall or may registers and rangers hold their appointments?

A. During good behaviour.

Q. Shall the sheriffs and coroners be commissioned?

A. Yes, by the governor.

Q. Shall registers, rangers, constables and trustees be commissioned?

A. The constitution does not absolutely require it.

Q. How many treasurers may there be in the state?

A. One or more.

Q. Who elects the treasurers?

A. The assembly, by joint ballot of both houses.

Q. How long may a treasurer hold his office?

A. Two years, and again eligible.

Q. Where the right of appointment is not directed by the constitution to be vested in the governor, or otherwise specially pointed out, who have the right of appointing?

A. In all such cases the assembly are vested with the power.

ARTICLE VII.

Q. How are captains, subalterns, and non-commissioned officers to be elected?

A. By those citizens in their respective districts who are subject to militia duty.

Q. How are field officers of the militia to be elected?

A. By those citizens in their respective counties who are subject to militia duty.

Q. How are brigadiers general elected?

A. By the field officers of the respective brigades.

Q. How are majors general to be elected?

A. By the brigadiers and field officers of their respective divisions.

Q. How is the adjutant general to be appointed?

A. By the governor.

Q. Who is to appoint aids to the majors general?

A. They are to be appointed by the majors general.

Q. Who is to appoint brigade majors?

A. The brigadiers general.

Q. Who is to appoint adjutants to regiments and quarter masters?

A. The commanding officers of regiments.

Q. How are the captains and subalterns of cavalry to be elected?

A. By the citizens of the respective companies.

Q. How are the field officers of cavalry to be elected?

A. By the captains and subalterns of the district.

Q. When a new county is laid off, who appoints the captain and other officers of cavalry?

A. The field officers of cavalry in the district shall appoint them, *pro tempore*, until the company is filled up, at which time, the election of the captains and subalterns shall be made in the usual way.

Q. Are citizens belonging to any religious sect, the tenets of which are known to be opposed to the bearing of arms, to be exempted from private and general musters?

A. The assembly shall pass laws to exempt them.

ARTICLE VIII.

Q. Are all ministers of the gospel, or priests of any denomination eligible to a seat in the legislature?

A. No.

Q. Can any citizen who denies the being of a God, or a future state of rewards and punishments, hold any office in the civil department of this state?

A. No.

ARTICLE IX.

Q. Are those who are appointed to any office of trust or profit required to take an oath before entering on the duties, and what is the tenor of such oath?

A. Yes; they shall take an oath to support the constitution, and also an oath of office.

Q. Are members of assembly required to take an oath before they proceed to business?

A. Yes; they shall take an oath to support the constitution of this state, and also the following oath: "I, *A. B.* do solemnly swear (or affirm) that as a member of this general assembly, I will in all appointments vote without favor, affection, partiality or prejudice; and that I will not propose, or assent to any bill, vote, or resolution which shall appear to me injurious to the people; or consent to any act or thing whatever, that shall have a tendency to lessen or abridge their rights and privileges, as declared by the constitution of this state."

Q. What is the tenor of the oath to be taken by the governor, before entering on the duties of his office?

A. An oath to support the constitution of this state, and of the United States, and also the following oath: "I *A. B.* do solemnly swear, that I will faithfully execute the office of governor of the state of Tennessee, pursuant to the constitution and laws thereof according to the best of my knowledge and ability. So help me God."

Q. Suppose an elector receives any gift, or reward for his vote, in meat, drink, money, or otherwise, shall he be punished?

A. Yes; in such way as the law shall direct.

Q. If any person shall directly or indirectly give, promise, or bestow a reward to be elected, is he punishable?

A. Yes; he shall be rendered incapable, for two years, to serve in the office to which he was elected, and be punished further as the assembly shall direct.

Q. Shall any county be divided, so as to leave the county off which the new one is taken, of less contents than six hundred and twenty five square miles?

A. No.

Q. Can any county be laid off of less contents than six hundred and twenty five square miles?

A. No.

Q. Are all new counties, as to the right of suffrage and representation, to be considered as a part of the old counties off which they were taken, until entitled by numbers to representation?

A. Yes.

Q. How is a new county to be obtained?

A. Upon petition to the assembly for that purpose, signed by two hundred of the free male inhabitants within the limits of such new county, prayed to be laid off.

ARTICLE X.

Q. Where shall the seat of government be?

A. At Knoxville, until the year 1802.

Q. Were all laws and ordinances in force and use in the Territory South of Ohio, enforced by this constitution, and how long were they to continue in force?

A. Yes; such as are not inconsistent with this constitution; and shall continue in force until they expire, are altered, or repealed by the legislature.

Q. Can this constitution be revised, amended, or changed, and how can it be effected?

A. When two thirds of the assembly think it necessary, they shall recommend it to the electors to vote for or against a convention, at their next election for members of assembly; and if it shall appear that a majority of all the citizens of the state, voting for representatives, have voted for a convention, the assembly shall, at their next session, call a convention.

Q. How many members shall compose that convention?

A. As many as compose the general assembly.

Q. How shall those members be elected?

A. In the same manner, at the same places, and by the same electors, that elected the assembly.

Q. Within what time shall the convention meet after the election?

A. Within three months.

Q. When met, how far may their powers extend?

A. To revising, amending, or changing the constitution.

Q. Is the declaration of rights declared to be a part of this constitution?

A. Yes, and it is said shall never be violated.

Q. Where is all power, not specially delegated by this constitution, vested?

A. In the people; and is excepted out of the general powers of government.

ARTICLE XI.
DECLARATION of RIGHTS.

Q. In whom is all power inherent?

A. In the people.

Q. On whose authority are all free governments founded?

A. On the authority of the people.

Q. For what purpose are free governments established?

A. For the peace, safety and happiness of the people.

Q. Have the people at all times an unalienable and indefeasible right to alter, reform, or abolish the government?

A. Yes, in such manner as they think proper.

Q. Is non resistance against arbitrary power and oppression absurd, slavish, and destructive to the good and happiness of mankind?

A. It is; because government is instituted for the common benefit of mankind.

Q. Have all men a natural and indefeasible right to worship Almighty God, according to the dictates of their own conscience?

A. Yes.

Q. Shall any man be compelled to attend, erect, or support any place of worship, or maintain any ministry against his consent?

A. No.

Q. Shall any preference be given by law to any religious establishment or mode of worship?

A. No.

Q. Shall any religious test ever be required as a qualification to any office, or public trust, under this state?

A. No.

Q. Shall all elections be free and equal?

A. Yes.

Q. Shall the trial by jury remain inviolate?

A. Yes.

Q. Shall people be secure in their persons, houses, papers and possessions from unreasonable searches and seizures?

A. Yes.

Q. Shall general warrants to search suspected places, without evidence of the fact committed, be granted?

A. No.

Q. Shall general warrants to seize any person not named, whose offences are not particularly described and supported by evidence, be granted?

A. No; they are dangerous to liberty.

Q. Shall any freeman be taken, or imprisoned, or disseized of his freehold, liberty or privileges, or outlawed, or exiled, or in any manner destroyed, or deprived of his life, liberty or property?

A. Not unless it be done by judgment of his peers, or the law of the land.

Q. How has the accused in criminal prosecutions a right to be heard?

A. By himself and by counsel.

Q. Has the accused a right to demand the nature

and cause of the accusation against him, and to have a copy thereof?

A. He has a right to demand.

Q. Has the accused a right to meet the witnesses face to face?

A. Yes.

Q. Has the accused a right to demand compulsory process for obtaining witnesses in his favor?

A. Yes.

Q. Has the accused a right to demand, in prosecutions by indictment or presentment, a speedy public trial, by an impartial jury of the county or district in which the crime shall have been committed?

A. Yes.

Q. Shall the accused be compelled to give evidence against himself?

A. No.

Q. Shall any person be twice put in jeopardy of life or limb for the same offence?

A. No.

Q. Shall laws be passed for the punishment of facts committed previous to the existence of such laws, and by them only declared to be criminal?

A. No.

Q. Shall any *ex post facto* law be made?

A. No.

Q. Shall the conviction of any criminal, work corruption of blood, or forfeiture of estate?

A. No.

Q. How shall the estates of such persons as destroy their own lives, descend or vest?

A. As in cases of natural death.

Q. If one person kills another casually, shall there be any forfeiture?

A. No.

Q. How shall a freeman be put to answer a criminal charge?

A. In no way, except by presentment, indictment or impeachment.

Q. Are all prisoners bailable by sufficient sureties?

A. Yes, unless for capital offences, when the proof is evident, or the presumption great.

Q. Shall the privilege of the writ of *Habeas Corpus* be suspended?

A. No; unless when in case of rebellion, or invasion, the public safety may require it.

Q. Shall excessive bail be required?

A. No.

Q. Shall excessive fines be imposed?

A. No.

Q. Shall cruel and unusal punishments be inflicted?

A. No.

Q. Shall all courts be open?

A. Yes.

Q. How shall a man, for an injury done him in his lands, goods, person, or reputation, have remedy?

A. By a due course of law.

Q. Shall right and justice be administered without denial or delay?

A. Yes.

Q. May this state be sued?

A. Yes.

Q. How may this state be sued?

A. In such manner, and in such courts as the general assembly may by law direct.

Q. Who has a right to sue this state?

A. None but a citizen of it.

Q. Shall a debtor be continued in prison, after he has delivered up his estate for the benefit of his creditors, as the law prescribes?

A. No, unlss there is strong presumption of fraud.

Q. Shall the printing presses be free to every person to examine the proceedings of the assembly, or of any branch or officer of government?

A. Yes.

Q. May any citizen freely speak, write, or print on any subject?

A. Yes; he being responsible for the abuse of that liberty.

Q. In prosecutions for publication against the official conduct of public officers, or men in public capacity, may the truth be given in evidence?

A. Yes.

Q. In all indictments for libels, shall the jury have a right to determine the law and the facts?

A. Yes, under the direction of the court, as in other cases.

Q. Shall any retrospective law, or law impairing the obligation of contracts, be made?

A. No.

Q. Shall any man's particular services be demanded, or property taken, or applied to public use?

A. Not without the consent of his representatives, or just compensation.

Q. Have the citizens a right, in a peaceable manner, to assemble for their common good, to instruct their representatives?

A. Yes.

Q. Have the citizens a right to apply to those who are invested with the powers of government, for redress of grievances?

A. Yes.

Q. Have the citizens a right to address or remonstrate generally?

A. Yes, respecting all proper purposes.

Q. Shall perpetuities and monopolies be allowed?

A. No.

Q. What is the sure and certain defence of a free people?

A. A well regulated militia.

Q. Shall standing armies in time of peace be avoided?

A. Yes, as far as circumstances, and the safety of the community will admit.

Q. Shall the military be in strict subordination to the civil authority?

A. Yes, in all cases.

Q. Shall any citizen be subject to corporal punishment, under the martial law?

A. No, except he is in the army of the United States, or militia in actual service.

Q. Have freemen a right to keep and bear arms?

A. Yes, for their common defence.

Q. Shall a soldier, in time of peace, be quartered in any house, without consent of the owner?

A. No.

Q. Shall a soldier, in time of war, be quartered in any house without consent of the owner?

A. In no other way than shall be prescribed by law.

Q. Shall a citizen be compelled to bear arms, if he will pay an equivalent?

A. No.

Q. How shall that equivalent be ascertained?

A. By law.

Q. Are the citizens of this state entitled to an equal participation of the free navigation of the Mississippi?

A. Yes.

Q. Shall any hereditary emoluments, privileges, or honors be granted or conferred in this state?

A. No.

Q. Are the people residing South of French Broad and Holston, between Tennessee and Big Pigeon, entitled to the right of pre emption and occupancy in that tract?

A. Yes, by this constitution.

Q. Are any other citizens entitled to pre emption claims on any other tract of country?

A. Not by this constitution.

Q. What are the boundaries and limits of this state?

A. By the declaration of rights they are declared to be as follow: "Beginning on the extreme height of the Stone Mountain, at the place where the Virginia line intersects it, in latitude thirty six degrees and thirty minutes North; running thence along the extreme height of the said Mountain, to the place where Watauga River breaks through it; thence a direct course to the top of the Yellow Mountain, where Bright's road crosses the same; thence along the ridge of said Mountain, between the waters of Doe River and the waters of Rock Creek, to the place where the road crosses the Iron Mountain; from thence along the extreme height of said Mountain, to where Nolichuckey River runs through the same; thence to the top of the Bald Mountain; thence along the extreme height of said Mountain to the Painted Rock on French Broad River; thence along the high ridge of said Mountain to the place where it is called the Great Iron or Smoky Mountain; thence along the extreme height of said Mountain to the place where it is called Unicoy or Unaka Mountain, between the Indian towns of Cowee and Old Chota; thence along the main ridge of the said Mountain, to the southern boundary of this state, as described in the act of cession of North Carolina, to the United States of America; and that all the territory, lands and waters, lying west of the said line, as before mentioned, and contained within the chartered limits of the state of North Carolina, are within the boundaries and limits of this state, over which the people have the right of exercising sovereignty and right of soil, so far as is consistent with the constitution of the United States, recognizing the articles of confederation, the bill of rights and constitution of North Carolina, the cession act of the said state, and the ordinance of the late Congress, for the government of the Territory North West of the Ohio: Provided, nothing herein contained, shall extend to affect the claim or claims of individuals to any part of the soil which is recognized to them by the aforesaid cession act."

SCHEDULE

Q. What kind of government existed within the limits of this state prior to the establishment of the constitution of Tennessee?

A. A Territorial Government, established under the authority of the United States.

Q. How was the inconvenience, which might be expected from the change of the temporary government to a permanent state government, guarded against?

A. It was declared by the convention, that all rights, actions, prosecutions, claims, and contracts should continue over, as if no change had taken place.

Q. What was done with all fines, forfeitures,

and penalties that were due to the Territorial Government?

A. It was declared that they should enure to the use of the state.

Q. What was done with all bonds for performance, executed to the Governor of the Territory?

A. It was declared that they should be and pass over to the Governor of this state, and his successors in office, for the use of the state; or by the Governor of the state, or his successors, to be assigned to those concerned, as the case might be.

Q. How long did the Governor, Secretary, Judges, and Brigadiers General, commissioned under the authority of the United States, continue to exercise their respective offices after the rise of the convention?

A. Until they were superceded under the authority of the constitution of Tennessee.

Q. How long did all officers, civil and military, who were appointed by the Territorial Governor, continue in their respective offices?

A. Until the second Monday in June, 1796, and until successors were appointed under the authority of the constitution of Tennessee, and were duly qualified.

Q. What seal was the Governor of Tennessee to use, until a seal was provided?

A. His private seal.

Q. How were members of assembly to be elected, prior to the first enumeration?

A. The people in each county were authorised to elect one senator and two representatives from each county.

Q. If new counties were laid off prior to the first enumeration, were they entitled to separate representation?

A. No; not until after the first enumeration.

Q. Where was the first election for representatives and other officers, held for the county of Tennessee, after the change of government?

A. At the house of William Miles.

Q. Are the citizens who reside South of French Broad and Holston, between Tennessee and Big Pigeon, who have claims to land by occupancy and pre emption, eligible to serve in all capacities, where a freehold is by the constitution made a requisite qualification?

A. Yes, until a land office shall be opened, to enable them to obtain titles to their lands.

THE END.